NEON SHAKESPEARE

❦

sonnets for a new millennium

by Joel Doerfel

Copyleft Ⓒ 2013 Long Yes Press

Published in the United States by Long Yes Press, longyespress@gmail.com.

Library of Congress Cataloging-in-Publication Data

Neon Shakespeare: Sonnets for a New Millennium / by Joel Doerfel
and William Shakespeare.

Includes endnotes and an index of first lines.
ISBN: 978-0-61565-840-7 (softcover : alk. paper)

1. Economic Awareness. In your revolutionary thinking, start with economics. 2.
Global citizen participation. 3. Social change—Global citizen participation. I.
Doerfel, Joel. II. Shakespeare, William.

table of contents

preface

I started this project in 1998 in an effort to get better at writing poetry. I was mainly writing free verse at the time, and wanted to teach myself some structure. So I wrote a sonnet in response to Shakespeare's first sonnet. Then I wrote another. And another. Seven years later, I had written 154 sonnets. *Neon Shakespeare* was born.

Over those seven years, I grew tremendously. Since I started at the beginning and wrote the sonnets (mostly) in order, the collection reflects my growth as a poet and thinker. Thus, the end of the collection contains my more recent, polished poetry, as well as my more recent philosophy. I recognize the risk of including early work in a first publication, but I ask my readers and reviewers for their magnanimity, given the ambition and scope of the project. The sonnets abound with lived observations, and my life has been profoundly changed through the process of writing them. What I say in Sonnet 101 applies to me:

an actor, you're the sum of all your parts.
your character is formed by roles you've played,
possessing bodies by this magic art—
the essence of the maker in the made.

Like Nietzsche's *Zarathustra*, this book of sonnets is truly "a book for all and none." Each sonnet is a stand-alone work of art. This book, then, can be read like a rhizome: picked up, put down, started, stopped, unplugged or plugged in anywhere readers desire. Stylistically and philosophically, these sonnets present a smorgasbord of literary delight. Some are absurd, some clever, some quirky, some nerdy, some academic, some conversational, some simple and soulful. These sonnets present such diversity that I imagine most readers will find many favorites.

Many of these sonnets are Shakespearean sonnets in classic form. Many are experimental. Experimentation ranges across every aspect of poetics—from letter, to syllable, to word, to foot, to meter, to line, to stanza, to poem, to poetic groupings, to discourse. Some devices found throughout are anagram, palindrome, and acrostic. Poetic experiments include abecedarius (23), multiple-meter (67), and additive letter poems (154).

This collection of sonnets is also rife with literary and philosophical allusions. Occasionally, a line or two will be presented in a foreign language (German, French, Italian, Latin, Ancient Greek, Ancient Hebrew or Aramaic). The "Notes" section in the rear of the book provides translations or references as needed, and occasionally alerts the reader to especially subtle experimental forms at play.

Notwithstanding, these sonnets are meant to be *interactive*. If you, my readers, imagine some play to be afoot, you're probably right. There are too many "easter eggs," allusions, and structural / linguistic / philosophical gems to annotate them all. The sonnets, then, besides being an enjoyable reading experience, are a vast ocean of logical twists and turns, a clever puzzle for inquisitive minds.

The sonnets are laid out with Shakespeare on the left-hand side of the page and my response sonnet on the right. Shakespeare calls, I respond. Since each of my sonnets is a conceptual response to its Shakespearean counterpart, readers are encouraged to read Shakespeare's sonnet first, followed by my response. My responses range from parody to commentary to elaboration to dumbfounded silence. Half the fun is unraveling the logic of this call-response.

My sonnets reflect my background in philosophy, language, history and the liberal arts. My sonnets also embody the fact that, as a sonneteer, I am self-trained. At least in the sense that I am a poet, Shakespeare is a philosopher. My hope is that pondering the logic of the call-response between my poems and Shakespeare's will motivate readers to treat Shakespeare's *philosophy* with the subtlety it merits. I hope this work occasions new readings of Shakespeare.

Since, as Isaac Newton once remarked, "we stand on the shoulders of giants," I'd like to thank my poetic forebears, especially Shakespeare, Neruda, Eliot, Saul Williams, and many of the poetic and philosophical ninjas who helped author what is now simply known as "The Bible." Philosophical thanks goes out to Heraclitus, Plato, Aristotle, Nietzsche, Heidegger, Foucault, and Deleuze / Guattari. Intellectual thanks to Douglas Hofstadter, whose avant-garde style in *Gödel, Escher, Bach* inspires the most technically rigorous, synesthetic, and recursive of the sonnets. Critical thanks to Helen Vendler for publishing the best English commentary available on Shakespeare's *Sonnets*.

Personally, I'd like to thank my academic teachers and mentors throughout the years, especially Dr. Kerry Magruder, Dr. William Dennison, Charles Dennison, Bob Madden, and Dr. Fred Evans. Warm thanks to Collin

Brack, Berto Legendary H, Carter Wallace and Vanessa Carlisle for help in making this publication a reality. A special thanks to my brother, James, for introducing me to poetry and for his sage advice throughout the years. A special thanks, as well, to Mariel Kyger for helping me prepare and publish this manuscript.

Finally, I'd like to thank all the wonderful patrons from Kickstarter who helped see this project into reality. A list of patrons appears on the next page. Thank you all, beautiful humans.

— *Los Angeles, 2012*

KICKSTARTER ACKNOWLEDGMENTS

Liz Ahl
Collin Brack
Mark Cason
Tylynn Chick
Anthony Cristofani
JoAnn DeSalvatore
Bill Doerfel
James Doerfel
Joanna Doerfel Thomson
Ryan Ellis
Eric Fholer
Sean Green
Berto Herrera
Rich Horton
Arthur Kay
Lisa Kinney
Sonia Koval
David Kyger
Mariel Kyger
Barbara Lindenmuth
Matt Lindenmuth
John Livingston
Marc Lombardo
Greg Malivuk
Elizabeth Marion
David Melville
Alan Moore
David Murray
Emily Olsen
Rick Quinn
Catherine Sandhofer
Chris Urban
Carter Wallace
Lori Wineman

sonnets

I

I.

FROM fairest creatures we desire increase,

That thereby beauty's rose might never die,

But as the riper should by time decease,

His tender heir might bear his memory:

But thou, contracted to thine own bright eyes,

Feed'st thy light'st flame with self-substantial fuel,

Making a famine where abundance lies,

Thyself thy foe, to thy sweet self too cruel.

Thou that art now the world's fresh ornament

And only herald to the gaudy spring,

Within thine own bud buriest thy content

And, tender churl, makest waste in niggarding.

Pity the world, or else this glutton be,

To eat the world's due, by the grave and thee.

~ WS

1

Your trembling petals when bedecked with dews,

Unfold sweet incense, vital instance of

Your dear perennial root. Whose life-lust woos

You fertile to this bed—except my love?

But you would not perpetuate your root;

You wrap your raiment tight about the fire

That burns within your bosom, making moot

Lush nature's boon with self-directed ire.

Your tender buds intrude spring's waking morn

Alone—except that I am here to lure

your heart. Your duty's filled if heirs are born

to us, or else death takes both you and your

whole race. O Rosebud, let your pasts and fut-

ures still bend to my will, and be not mute.

~ JD

II.

When forty winters shall beseige thy brow,

And dig deep trenches in thy beauty's field,

Thy youth's proud livery, so gazed on now,

Will be a tatter'd weed, of small worth held:

Then being ask'd where all thy beauty lies,

Where all the treasure of thy lusty days,

To say, within thine own deep-sunken eyes,

Were an all-eating shame and thriftless praise.

How much more praise deserved thy beauty's use,

If thou couldst answer 'This fair child of mine

Shall sum my count and make my old excuse,'

Proving his beauty by succession thine!

This were to be new made when thou art old,

And see thy blood warm when thou feel'st it cold.

~ WS

2

The tessellated snowflake lands its slender
Crystal mass upon the heft of snow-
Drift covering your heart, and softly ends
Your muffled sobs, these memoirs to so

Long ago, remembrances of beauty.
Where is the lusty shepherdess, with her
Olive skin, her dark and flashing eyes? She,
Swept by time, though aged, is bringing order

To the world by birth. Rejoice O earth! The
mantle of her Grace has passed to Heir. Why
then, does she exclaim, now dying there, "He
is my Son of Sorrow?" Shall sand or sky

Memorialize her path? Shall sky or sand?
I name her child: "My Son, of My Right Hand."

~ JD

III.

Look in thy glass, and tell the face thou viewest

Now is the time that face should form another;

Whose fresh repair if now thou not renewest,

Thou dost beguile the world, unbless some mother.

For where is she so fair whose unear'd womb

Disdains the tillage of thy husbandry?

Or who is he so fond will be the tomb

Of his self-love, to stop posterity?

Thou art thy mother's glass, and she in thee

Calls back the lovely April of her prime:

So thou through windows of thine age shall see

Despite of wrinkles this thy golden time.

But if thou live, remember'd not to be,

Die single, and thine image dies with thee.

~ WS

3

Look in this pool—within the face you're viewing

Lie latent generations. The lines and

Hidden veins lie fallow there, renewing

A harvest if someone but plow their land.

The golden leaves surround you as you stare

At your reflection in the pond...warm breeze

And longing shadows make you pause, despair,

Cling tightly to the vital root you seize.

Companions fall headlong to earth—thus orbs

Life's cycling way. Who strives against time's flow?

The silly, paranoid and self-absorbed

Harbor fears of natural anaestha.

So leaf, fall to my lap; die in my bed—

Your fruit will live long after you are dead.

~ JD

IV.

Unthrifty loveliness, why dost thou spend

Upon thyself thy beauty's legacy?

Nature's bequest gives nothing but doth lend,

And being frank she lends to those are free.

Then, beauteous niggard, why dost thou abuse

The bounteous largess given thee to give?

Profitless usurer, why dost thou use

So great a sum of sums, yet canst not live?

For having traffic with thyself alone,

Thou of thyself thy sweet self dost deceive.

Then how, when nature calls thee to be gone,

What acceptable audit canst thou leave?

Thy unused beauty must be tomb'd with thee,

Which, used, lives th' executor to be.

~ WS

4

Beautiful you. You stand on the banks of
Posterity. They woo your prize with lowered
Rates. "Invest! Make babies, making love.
Through them live on! Here, by the river, sow!"

The Ancient Life-flow either lends or gives.
It lends to those who spend it on themselves—
(Within the "progeny-investor" lives
The self-spendthrift, who into life-debt delves.)

Mammon's curse bests that of Tantalus' fruit—
Riches can be held in hand, but you may
Only *own* all that your left hand can pay
Your right—a maze with only one way out:

Become the river's love: give life, don't lend.
The Audit's goal is Nothing in the end.

~ JD

V.

Those hours, that with gentle work did frame

The lovely gaze where every eye doth dwell,

Will play the tyrants to the very same

And that unfair which fairly doth excel:

For never-resting time leads summer on

To hideous winter and confounds him there;

Sap cheque'd with frost and lusty leaves quite gone,

Beauty o'ersnow'd and bareness every where:

Then, were not summer's distillation left,

A liquid prisoner pent in walls of glass,

Beauty's effect with beauty were bereft,

Nor it nor no remembrance what it was:

But flowers distill'd though they with winter meet,

Leese but their show; their substance still lives sweet.

~ WS

5

'Tick...tick...drip...drip...' sings your spring of beauty—
gurgling, rushing, sweeping suitors as it
goes—though each knows it flows to dark exit,
and 'tock | tock-drop' will stop eventually.

Fate-cadence trades his scythe in for syringe
named 'entropy:' now world feels winter as
his cool, his clinic-hands caress, anaes-
thetize, and softly shroud earth's every fringe

with white. Cold calculus! See medic-time,
with martial step, march down chill, sterile hall,
with frigid breath last drops of spring to stall,
encasing all in his Cryogeny.

...But madness smiles its champion enzyme,
As spring erupts insane in: "progeny!"

~ JD

VI.

Then let not winter's ragged hand deface

In thee thy summer, ere thou be distill'd:

Make sweet some vial; treasure thou some place

With beauty's treasure, ere it be self-kill'd.

That use is not forbidden usury,

Which happies those that pay the willing loan;

That's for thyself to breed another thee,

Or ten times happier, be it ten for one;

Ten times thyself were happier than thou art,

If ten of thine ten times refigured thee:

Then what could death do, if thou shouldst depart,

Leaving thee living in posterity?

Be not self-will'd, for thou art much too fair

To be death's conquest and make worms thine heir.

~ WS

6

To catch this catalyst? It's harder than
It seems! For lunacy admits no for-
gery. This liquid prey slips, mocks pandor-
a's box, and eludes each vial of human

will that would distill its treasure. So pro-
create! ...Invest! Your quest for permanence
wields winter's art but poorly! Trapped or fro-
zen? Not even slowed! Life's drip-drop Non-sense

baits you to calculate: "...Maybe 'Ten' of
you could catch me better than one! What could
death do then?" ...Soft Death's foot-falls find a hood
in every season. ...as do Life's! For cov-

ered by *your* ratiocination, Time's
crazy oblation laughs Life-giving crimes.

~ JD

VII.

Lo! in the orient when the gracious light

Lifts up his burning head, each under eye

Doth homage to his new-appearing sight,

Serving with looks his sacred majesty;

And having climb'd the steep-up heavenly hill,

Resembling strong youth in his middle age,

yet mortal looks adore his beauty still,

Attending on his golden pilgrimage;

But when from highmost pitch, with weary car,

Like feeble age, he reeleth from the day,

The eyes, 'fore duteous, now converted are

From his low tract and look another way:

So thou, thyself out-going in thy noon,

Unlook'd on diest, unless thou get a son.

~ WS

7

Look to the Orient where soft-red dawns
The fiery emperor. New eyes flash bright
To greet his life-engend'ring gaze. Each fawns
On him, genuflects to his morning-light.

This gen'rous nourisher ascends as sire;
His potency has flourished in his prime:
And mortal offspring-multitudes admire
Their royal head in this his golden time.

But when from noon of strength he tumbles down,
His crimson eye grows dim, no more sustains
His parasitic wards, his hordes, no long-
er fed, turn scarlet proletarians.

So thou, before thou think'st to get a son,
Look on thy waning, more than this thy noon.

~ JD

VIII.

Music to hear, why hear'st thou music sadly?

Sweets with sweets war not, joy delights in joy.

Why lovest thou that which thou receivest not gladly,

Or else receivest with pleasure thine annoy?

If the true concord of well-tuned sounds,

By unions married, do offend thine ear,

They do but sweetly chide thee, who confounds

In singleness the parts that thou shouldst bear.

Mark how one string, sweet husband to another,

Strikes each in each by mutual ordering,

Resembling sire and child and happy mother

Who all in one, one pleasing note do sing:

Whose speechless song, being many, seeming one,

Sings this to thee: 'thou single wilt prove none.'

~ WS

8

Music? My bow has hovered o'er your strings,
Has teased your chords of heart toward fruition…
So now we two are coupled (of all things!)
And 'harmony' comes forth from our coition.

'The music of the spheres'? Our orbs are crossed!
(When she's in March, I'm still in May; my June
is her December!) …Undulation-tossed,
her rhythm rides but never fits my tune.

For Tempo's taut cacophonies resound
Within our souls with every revolution.
Amid its strains and symphonies we're bound—
Its tension-chords that show no resolution.

We theorize our civil Chaos-specks—
But resonate the cosmic strife of sex.

~ JD

IX.

Is it for fear to wet a widow's eye

That thou consumest thyself in single life?

Ah! if thou issueless shalt hap to die.

The world will wail thee, like a makeless wife;

The world will be thy widow and still weep

That thou no form of thee hast left behind,

When every private widow well may keep

By children's eyes her husband's shape in mind.

Look, what an unthrift in the world doth spend

Shifts but his place, for still the world enjoys it;

But beauty's waste hath in the world an end,

And kept unused, the user so destroys it.

No love toward others in that bosom sits

That on himself such murderous shame commits.

~ WS

9

Come dance with me, spider! Why do you cow-
er in the shadows? You are a shame to
both your race and species: your race's pow-
er lies dormant in your silky womb—you

have spun no web. As species: do you fear
to brave sunlight as a widow or as black?
You counterfeit recluse! Come out my dear,
And ply your magic arts; stretch taut your slack-

ened cords; allure, seduce, intoxicate
your prey. Fight, blight, or tight-wire height can make
the world your widow—as can hesitat-
ing—either way death's mystic web will take

you. Spread a silken bed to tease this fly:
if you can't suck my juice, you'll starve and die.

~ JD

X.

For shame! deny that thou bear'st love to any,

Who for thyself art so unprovident.

Grant, if thou wilt, thou art beloved of many,

But that thou none lovest is most evident;

For thou art so possess'd with murderous hate

That 'gainst thyself thou stick'st not to conspire.

Seeking that beauteous roof to ruinate

Which to repair should be thy chief desire.

O, change thy thought, that I may change my mind!

Shall hate be fairer lodged than gentle love?

Be, as thy presence is, gracious and kind,

Or to thyself at least kind-hearted prove:

Make thee another self, for love of me,

That beauty still may live in thine or thee.

~ WS

10

For Shame! Not Anger, Guilt or Pride, nor sad
Fatigue nor black Melancholy; but Shame
draws on your thoughts toward self-demise. Kaleid-
oscoping cosmos scabs your conscience, maims

bold reverence into shy "modesty."
Is this "modesty" some harmless under-
valuation? No! See your self-worth reach
forth gaunt, emaciated arms; seek from

you with final gasp its food. Let it not
be resign, then, that allows me near
to whisper here, "unbuyable...unbought;"
rather, feed your Honor; align her star-

ry eyes with mine; forego this dreadful deed;
and in my Line let your beauty's Life be read.

~ JD

XI.

As fast as thou shalt wane, so fast thou growest

In one of thine, from that which thou departest;

And that fresh blood which youngly thou bestowest

Thou mayst call thine when thou from youth convertest.

Herein lives wisdom, beauty and increase:

Without this, folly, age and cold decay:

If all were minded so, the times should cease

And threescore year would make the world away.

Let those whom Nature hath not made for store,

Harsh featureless and rude, barrenly perish:

Look, whom she best endow'd she gave the more;

Which bounteous gift thou shouldst in bounty cherish:

She carved thee for her seal, and meant thereby

Thou shouldst print more, not let that copy die.

~ WS

11

Days dawn on all, and sweet rains fall unbi-

asedly to earth. Soft soils yield their man-

ifold: young, lovely, ripe and firm...supply-

ing life as well to blighted, ugly, and

malformed; to weak and over-ripe. Kind earth gives

power of birth to each, and "selects" none. Those

who are "prime" repress the times and spaces

of their lack, and pretend that their strength goes

unchanged through Nature's turns. What then will come,

my love, from our alloy? Plush today; to-

morrow plain. Lusty, lush deflowering moons

recycle to dawn's floral pyre. Love, do

we mix our love-petals with deeper weeds and dead?

I love you. Pass my wine. Let's go to bed.

~ JD

XII.

When I do count the clock that tells the time,

And see the brave day sunk in hideous night;

When I behold the violet past prime,

And sable curls all silver'd o'er with white;

When lofty trees I see barren of leaves

Which erst from heat did canopy the herd,

And summer's green all girded up in sheaves

Borne on the bier with white and bristly beard,

Then of thy beauty do I question make,

That thou among the wastes of time must go,

Since sweets and beauties do themselves forsake

And die as fast as they see others grow;

And nothing 'gainst Time's scythe can make defence

Save breed, to brave him when he takes thee hence.

~ WS

when worlds tick to my java-eddy spoons
and red cells cycle after evening pleasure;
when hazy purple hot flash autumn moons
sound silent gray-haired geezers' final measure;

when twisters penetrating soils pluck muds,
sweep over harvests, dissolve to muffle
prairie-plaints, gust to shudder-thuds,
jet-hurricane, overseas-unruffle—

then, my love, the cosmos and i will knock;
for in your womb throbs all of this and more;
your fertile seed-bed rhythms trump the clock:
world-pulse demands that you be bride or whore.

the wind is coming, and you know not whence.
choose bride; before our spirits blend askance.

~ JD

XIII.

O, that you were yourself! but, love, you are

No longer yours than you yourself here live:

Against this coming end you should prepare,

And your sweet semblance to some other give.

So should that beauty which you hold in lease

Find no determination: then you were

Yourself again after yourself's decease,

When your sweet issue your sweet form should bear.

Who lets so fair a house fall to decay,

Which husbandry in honour might uphold

Against the stormy gusts of winter's day

And barren rage of death's eternal cold?

O, none but unthrifts! Dear my love, you know

You had a father: let your son say so.

~ WS

the earth and all generations are your

skin, your house; every famine, every

blight, tilts the scale (however slightly)

of your being: your smell, toenail color

and melatonin level...somehow tied

to whether some forebear ate mangos on

september 21, 1801.

inside each woven body-fiber hides

the world—nature overlaid with human

order; man's markets sort formed-muds into

lovelies and uglies. just your luck, dear, to

wear the name "lovely"! now not only can

you recycle progeny and/or stardust,

but also (think of it!) "beauty" (and "lust").

~ JD

XIV.

Not from the stars do I my judgment pluck;

And yet methinks I have astronomy,

But not to tell of good or evil luck,

Of plagues, of deaths, or seasons' quality;

Nor can I fortune to brief minutes tell,

Pointing to each his thunder, rain and wind,

Or say with princes if it shall go well,

By oft predict that I in heaven find:

But from thine eyes my knowledge I derive,

And, constant stars, in them I read such art

As truth and beauty shall together thrive,

If from thyself to store thou wouldst convert;

Or else of thee this I prognosticate:

Thy end is truth's and beauty's doom and date.

~ WS

14

night-swimming sky-vault summer pangs past
milky rivulets. young love hot purling
pisces purple moon-tide memory. vast
sea green grass churn castaways on rafting

blanket-lust...now buried in some murky
swirl-recess-lost-lore of shade spent ener-
gy. fight fish! thrash, flail impaled on dark sea-
soul; twist, lash on myth-hook, guilt-line-surge:

foam-fear, misunderstood submerge; dive, con-
fused, too deep. fem-fatigue, surf-surface float
spent flounder-breasts. ...strained cords bore us paired in-
to this torch-lit state (burning in me), this blue sky-boat.

our tension, cold, coy fish, holds taut all species—
subconscious *oikos* of the 12th chromatic tone.

~ JD

XV.

When I consider every thing that grows

Holds in perfection but a little moment,

That this huge stage presenteth nought but shows

Whereon the stars in secret influence comment;

When I perceive that men as plants increase,

Cheered and cheque'd even by the self-same sky,

Vaunt in their youthful sap, at height decrease,

And wear their brave state out of memory;

Then the conceit of this inconstant stay

Sets you most rich in youth before my sight,

Where wasteful Time debateth with Decay,

To change your day of youth to sullied night;

And all in war with Time for love of you,

As he takes from you, I engraft you new.

~ WS

15.

when photosynthesizing next to you

amid bright frosty dews and frozen loams

or turning O_2 into CO_2

as crickets croon last lyric sultry poems;

when sacrificing leaf or limb to some

furry, feathered, or scaly partner in

our biosphere, or eating fresh-laid dung

or drinking rain, or watching heavens spin,

then i muse: can eagle mate with swan;

canine with bull? what hybrid then could grow

from weed and flower? must you be pollin-

ated? will it have been enough to know

your scent, be rooted in your minerals,

not knowing what is annual or perennial?

~ JD

XVI.

But wherefore do not you a mightier way

Make war upon this bloody tyrant, Time?

And fortify yourself in your decay

With means more blessed than my barren rhyme?

Now stand you on the top of happy hours,

And many maiden gardens yet unset

With virtuous wish would bear your living flowers,

Much liker than your painted counterfeit:

So should the lines of life that life repair,

Which this, Time's pencil, or my pupil pen,

Neither in inward worth nor outward fair,

Can make you live yourself in eyes of men.

To give away yourself keeps yourself still,

And you must live, drawn by your own sweet skill.

~ WS

16.

blood-speckled leaves of times must rustle at

advance of sword & pen (hills, seas, & stars?)

—ink globules staining ream & stem forget

how parastigmatic hemogoblins wing over waters,

sing; haunt day-dreams; cling to absent chores. just so

will science smart both head & heart till cacti ooze red

jelly increments onto vast tracts of lone-

ly clay (excremental, sun-baked, cackling muds

with sands for hands when moon-clouds drip their

day); where feral equine rife range over luminal voids—

till pressed to serve the chariot-wheels of mechanic per-

iod in sapient parodyxical parade

they jape their neigh to tactile desert reins:

ut velis mutari ab arte in memoriam!

~ JD

XVII.

Who will believe my verse in time to come,

If it were fill'd with your most high deserts?

Though yet, heaven knows, it is but as a tomb

Which hides your life and shows not half your parts.

If I could write the beauty of your eyes

And in fresh numbers number all your graces,

The age to come would say 'This poet lies:

Such heavenly touches ne'er touch'd earthly faces.'

So should my papers yellow'd with their age

Be scorn'd like old men of less truth than tongue,

And your true rights be term'd a poet's rage

And stretched metre of an antique song:

But were some child of yours alive that time,

You should live twice; in it and in my rhyme.

~ WS

17.

i'm sure

you shall

endure

for all

i need

to do

is breed

with you

then pen

your name

to win

you fame

pass the

womb please

~ JD

XVIII.

Shall I compare thee to a summer's day?

Thou art more lovely and more temperate:

Rough winds do shake the darling buds of May,

And summer's lease hath all too short a date:

Sometime too hot the eye of heaven shines,

And often is his gold complexion dimm'd;

And every fair from fair sometime declines,

By chance or nature's changing course untrimm'd;

But thy eternal summer shall not fade,

Nor lose possession of that fair thou owest;

Nor shall Death brag thou wander'st in his shade,

When in eternal lines to time thou growest:

So long as men can breathe or eyes can see,

So long lives this, and this gives life to thee.

~ WS

18

Death thou art untrimmed, and owest all to
the eternal fade of Time. So too thou
growest thy Gold but by his lease. Do
the eyes of men see thee, thou eternal

too-dimmed Day, changing Nature's possession?
So summer shines...and Shade shall shake every
fair Darling to rough and hot complexion;
nor shall buds breathe more, nor sometime-lovely

May brag temperate. Sometime when thou wand-
erest in from summer's winds, Chance shall compare
Heaven to this life, that of-a-course declines, and
date this summer's long Fair, more fair

short. I long often and lose lives (as is in His eye)—
He: a 'can'? 'cannot'? or hath lines? or gives thee?

~ JD

XIX.

Devouring Time, blunt thou the lion's paws,

And make the earth devour her own sweet brood;

Pluck the keen teeth from the fierce tiger's jaws,

And burn the long-lived phoenix in her blood;

Make glad and sorry seasons as thou fleets,

And do whate'er thou wilt, swift-footed Time,

To the wide world and all her fading sweets;

But I forbid thee one most heinous crime:

O, carve not with thy hours my love's fair brow,

Nor draw no lines there with thine antique pen;

Him in thy course untainted do allow

For beauty's pattern to succeeding men.

Yet, do thy worst, old Time: despite thy wrong,

My love shall in my verse ever live young.

~ WS

19.

clear-flowing time, turn gem to dust and back;

choke species with your incremental rain;

freeze lava core to cold, dark, lonely rock;

unravel quarks, mute matter once again.

erode four-fielded force; gurgle among

electrons. drown alphabets; wash grammars

in your wake. waste walls & myths & bones

& souls of men. but unseen flood, take your

flu from things divine. aspire not to

touch eternity. if these be in your

grasp, then what is man? (no more ask "who?")

if god's in flux, what meaning has the word?

concede: if time makes talk ephemeral,

brides, gods—these words—won't last millennia.

XX.

A woman's face with Nature's own hand painted

Hast thou, the master-mistress of my passion;

A woman's gentle heart, but not acquainted

With shifting change, as is false women's fashion;

An eye more bright than theirs, less false in rolling,

Gilding the object whereupon it gazeth;

A man in hue, all 'hues' in his controlling,

Much steals men's eyes and women's souls amazeth.

And for a woman wert thou first created;

Till Nature, as she wrought thee, fell a-doting,

And by addition me of thee defeated,

By adding one thing to my purpose nothing.

But since she prick'd thee out for women's pleasure,

Mine be thy love and thy love's use their treasure.

~ WS

20

my jungle jury echoes, "onan...o...."

the whales object; I cry, "a cross, orca!"

lizards hiss...I: *"sodom*, o komodos!"

(Peux-tu pénétrer l'homme, o bonobo?)

"A banana, thanks; some water, bless you.

...why this kindness?" (weeping) "You're the only...

Why, I could just kiss..." Strange that I blush; why...

love, respect, friendship...sex—*who made these to*

share a syntax? "Am I a beast?!?" I roar.

"Am I a god?" ripostes a chimp, *"Power*

speaks through blood: lineage, analysis, war;

birth, cycles, Death...."   ...I wake to sweat, sheets wet;

my muse is lost. the moon is full. I am

the waves. Who's in my bed? A historian?

~ JD

XXI.

So is it not with me as with that Muse
Stirr'd by a painted beauty to his verse,
Who heaven itself for ornament doth use
And every fair with his fair doth rehearse

Making a couplement of proud compare,
With sun and moon, with earth and sea's rich gems,
With April's first-born flowers, and all things rare
That heaven's air in this huge rondure hems.

O' let me, true in love, but truly write,
And then believe me, my love is as fair
As any mother's child, though not so bright
As those gold candles fix'd in heaven's air:

Let them say more than like of hearsay well;
I will not praise that purpose not to sell.

~ WS

21

Call me Nature's copyist. All I do

is translate your beauty, pixel by pix-

el onto poetic canvas, onto

this page. I'm a realist. I squirt and mix

dyes on my palette. I'm honest. I don't

flatter. Posterity will see you *wie*

du eigentlich gewesen bist. You can't

deny the flawless adequation. See?

I'm a scientist! I don't use hyper-

bole, metaphor, or analogy.

My lens is not soft-focused. You under-

stand? Straight talk. That's my game. Now where were we?

Oh yes...brown hair...brown eyes.... (I won't stop un-

til I've exhausted your description!) ...chin...

~ JD

XXII.

My glass shall not persuade me I am old,

So long as youth and thou are of one date;

But when in thee time's furrows I behold,

Then look I death my days should expiate.

For all that beauty that doth cover thee

Is but the seemly raiment of my heart,

Which in thy breast doth live, as thine in me:

How can I then be elder than thou art?

O, therefore, love, be of thyself so wary

As I, not for myself, but for thee will;

Bearing thy heart, which I will keep so chary

As tender nurse her babe from faring ill.

Presume not on thy heart when mine is slain;

Thou gavest me thine, not to give back again.

~ WS

22.

We've grown so close in love that I don't know

If in our breasts there beats one heart or two.

Each day I wake to sense your Gem-in-eyes,

Ambrosia hair, soft cheeks and neck and face.

I wish that love would melt us into one...

But there you stand, naked Me, as handsome

As ever, gazing back at I from your

Mirror universe. Ay Me! Not grammar

merely keeps I from saying, "I am Me."

I see; Me's seen. I act, though my sweet Me be

acted on! I love you, Me! I love, I

guess, what others see. In fact, Me guards my

heart, I his... ...till we attract self-image?

Gay three-some, psycho-trinity: I, *Myself*, & Me.

~ JD

II

XXIII.

As an unperfect actor on the stage

Who with his fear is put besides his part,

Or some fierce thing replete with too much rage,

Whose strength's abundance weakens his own heart.

So I, for fear of trust, forget to say

The perfect ceremony of love's rite,

And in mine own love's strength seem to decay,

O'ercharged with burden of mine own love's might.

O, let my looks[1] be then the eloquence

And dumb presagers of my speaking breast,

Who plead for love and look for recompense

More than that tongue that more hath more express'd.

O, learn to read what silent love hath writ:

To hear with eyes belongs to love's fine wit.

---

[1] alt. books

~ WS

23.

a bashful coed's dancing eyebrows flirt,

giggle (heart-in-jugular). karma lingers.

mouths never open. ...pause.... queasy, rumbling

stomachs tell unspoken valedictions,

wild ecstasy, yearnfilled zen. meet me

at the windows for my soul—panes where in-

ward being bends toward mankind, pines (chin-

in-palms) for its mate. crack the casement, then,

that there we might share selves by a mass of

air. earth-tone, moon-strain, shadow-pitches rise.

when we extrospect, we enter entirities.

so over the roof we go—go over to the wet torpor of

the tree (of the root, of the top) oh... oh... oh...

over the roof of the fog, of the ore, the roe: to the abode.

~ JD

XXIV.

Mine eye hath play'd the painter and hath stell'd

Thy beauty's form in table of my heart;

My body is the frame wherein 'tis held,

And perspective it is the painter's art.

For through the painter must you see his skill,

To find where your true image pictured lies;

Which in my bosom's shop is hanging still,

That hath his windows glazed with thine eyes.

Now see what good turns eyes for eyes have done:

Mine eyes have drawn thy shape, and thine for me

Are windows to my breast, where-through the sun

Delights to peep, to gaze therein on thee;

Yet eyes this cunning want to grace their art;

They draw but what they see, know not the heart.

~ WS

24.

still life fruit evil good of knowing you.
i reflect you in your room, that day we
became one fleshy pigment, fibrous fruit,
lifeless mirror-image. you complete me,

reverse me, completely reverse me. we're two—
strife-drawn together, ink-ionized to face each
other's dusty shadow-sides; some elsewhere
eros-fall your faded sunny tints, secret juices,

tones (tains?) of warm bare skin. we're one—
how could i cast myself to shards? slice you, and i
am sliced. together we're crackled, torn, or smudged.
so stretch us tight around the frame and staple us.

we lie flat and frigid. taut canvas dyed serene.
knowing of good. evil life fruit. still you.

~ JD

XXV.

Let those who are in favour with their stars

Of public honour and proud titles boast,

Whilst I, whom fortune of such triumph bars,

Unlook'd for joy in that I honour most.

Great princes' favourites their fair leaves spread

But as the marigold at the sun's eye,

And in themselves their pride lies buried,

For at a frown they in their glory die.

The painful warrior famoused for fight,

After a thousand victories once foil'd,

Is from the book of honour razed quite,

And all the rest forgot for which he toil'd:

Then happy I, that love and am beloved

Where I may not remove nor be removed.

~ WS

25.

LET KINGS & SOLDIERS PEN THEIR HISTORIES

& PUT ON HEIRS & SPAWN THEIR AVATARS;

RAISE MONUMENTS; ISSUE EDICTS: *SEMEN*

SCIENTIAE SANGUINA FABRĪ EST.

BUT WHERE WILL OUR LOVE BE SKETCHED?

ON FADED BODY-SCROLLS? WHAT BLOOD WILL SEAL

OUR MARRIAGE PACT? MENSTRUAL? PLACENTAL?

CERTAINLY THESE, BUT MEN DON'T BLEED LIKE THAT.

WE ONLY BLEED FOR WOUNDS OR WAR OR DEATH...

...AND EACH OF THESE MIGHT HARM OR END OUR LOVE!

SO I MUST SIGN WITH HIGHER ELEMENTS—

ETHEREAL INK FROM CLOUDY WELLS ABOVE.

I'LL SHARE MY AIRY VEINS—A MYTHIC LIFE.

I'LL SIGN THUS. SIGN WITH BLOOD. BECOME MY WIFE.

~ JD

XXVI.

Lord of my love, to whom in vassalage

Thy merit hath my duty strongly knit,

To thee I send this written embassage,

To witness duty, not to show my wit:

Duty so great, which wit so poor as mine

May make seem bare, in wanting words to show it,

But that I hope some good conceit of thine

In thy soul's thought, all naked, will bestow it;

Till whatsoever star that guides my moving

Points on me graciously with fair aspect

And puts apparel on my tatter'd loving,

To show me worthy of thy sweet respect:

Then may I dare to boast how I do love thee;

Till then not show my head where thou mayst prove me.

~ WS

26.

o domina, dicte et facam quod

amabas. fac me, canis! asper! sic!

master or slave? ...depends on what position

we assume. love takes root below such differences

and grows above them. but it does grow through them.

our passion swells and strains these definitions,

a thing too big to fit into its place.

just so, babies stretch-fit through labiae;

your heart through mind; my tenderness through words.

our shared elation mounts through dormant vows.

i cherish you tight-through few memories.

you, nude, stretch/play through/in victorian shame.

of course, one other thing has grown so great...

dare you stretch-open lips to master it?

~ JD

XXVII.

Weary with toil, I haste me to my bed,

The dear repose for limbs with travel tired;

But then begins a journey in my head,

To work my mind, when body's work's expired:

For then my thoughts, from far where I abide,

Intend a zealous pilgrimage to thee,

And keep my drooping eyelids open wide,

Looking on darkness which the blind do see

Save that my soul's imaginary sight

Presents thy shadow to my sightless view,

Which, like a jewel hung in ghastly night,

Makes black night beauteous and her old face new.

Lo! thus, by day my limbs, by night my mind,

For thee and for myself no quiet find.

~ WS

27.

working the soil as dawn's red lord ascends,

my bare black back prepares to feel his fire.

dark bugsongs, sore sinews, and sleepy eyes

swap customary nods, trampled commune

amid dim furrows, barren bond without

you. a saline universe trickles down

my brow and falls to wrinkled earth. For one

instant i am, i sail a sea of sweat

for you...then soak into the brown. i am

a reservoir of notes that never find

you. even when the soul of twilight drowns

the sun and i'd make me an ocean from

tears, dust-devils drink me. all gods are liars—

bright sun and black earth muffle my desires.

~ JD

XXVIII.

How can I then return in happy plight,

That am debarr'd the benefit of rest?

When day's oppression is not eased by night,

But day by night, and night by day, oppress'd?

And each, though enemies to either's reign,

Do in consent shake hands to torture me;

The one by toil, the other to complain

How far I toil, still farther off from thee.

I tell the day, to please them thou art bright

And dost him grace when clouds do blot the heaven:

So flatter I the swart-complexion'd night,

When sparkling stars tire not thou gild'st the even.

But day doth daily draw my sorrows longer

And night doth nightly make grief's strength seem stronger.

~ WS

28.

this web of nerves is our intelligence—

this net of eyes & ears, nose, mouth, & skin.

our sapience: symbolic sentience.

our minds are not just tenants of our brains.

but if we shift our wit to silicon,

(while hedonists roll over in their graves),

whose victory lives on once flesh is gone?

& what will have escaped from plato's cave?

the more we change, the more we stay the same.

the ancient quest for immortality

is echoed in each generation's games—

myth, photograph, e-personality.

today, we write and read ideas aloud.

tonight, your soul's uploaded to the cloud.

~ JD

XXIX.

When, in disgrace with fortune and men's eyes,

I all alone beweep my outcast state,

And trouble deaf heaven with my bootless cries,

And look upon myself and curse my fate,

Wishing me like to one more rich in hope,

Featured like him, like him with friends possess'd,

Desiring this man's art and that man's scope,

With what I most enjoy contented least;

Yet in these thoughts myself almost despising,

Haply I think on thee, and then my state,

Like to the lark at break of day arising

From sullen earth, sings hymns at heaven's gate;

For thy sweet love remember'd such wealth brings

That then I scorn to change my state with kings.

~ WS

29.

Can any man cross Jahweh's changeless will?

"I AM" shakes pear extract from plums, water

from rocks, bread from dew (enough to feed mill-

ions). His voice strips forests bare...calves from deer.

A host shouts "Glory!" in his house. It's He,

the Torah-story says, who rules our fate—

money, health, genius, self-esteem, beauty—

He gives us more or less, and sets the date

and hour of our death. We grow together,

you and I, like two flowers. And sometimes

when you hold me, I forget my brother's

suicide, or what the *Religions-*

geschictlicheschule found. And sometimes

not. And I am happy. And I love you.

~ JD

XXX.

When to the sessions of sweet silent thought

I summon up remembrance of things past,

I sigh the lack of many a thing I sought,

And with old woes new wail my dear time's waste:

Then can I drown an eye, unused to flow,

For precious friends hid in death's dateless night,

And weep afresh love's long since cancell'd woe,

And moan the expense of many a vanish'd sight:

Then can I grieve at grievances foregone,

And heavily from woe to woe tell o'er

The sad account of fore-bemoaned moan,

Which I new pay as if not paid before.

But if the while I think on thee, dear friend,

All losses are restored and sorrows end.

30.

when some wet lore-drop surfaces to thought,
or yore-trace blows in, or molten memory
churns up, and i find myself apparent
heir to some recycled ego-vestige:

then i can smile, or dread, or follow a
routine; regret a lost cause, or find my
keys; or cut through a sleepy fog via
metempsychosis to re-become "i;"

then i can flee the *götzendämmerung*
of waking life for the phantasmagor-
ia of dreams (here memory functions too)—
remembering is the glue of my lifeworld.

but your ghost, late friend, dissolves its milieu:
en toi, mémoire et temps sont tous perdus.

~ JD

XXXI.

Thy bosom is endeared with all hearts,

Which I by lacking have supposed dead,

And there reigns love and all love's loving parts,

And all those friends which I thought buried.

How many a holy and obsequious tear

Hath dear religious love stol'n from mine eye

As interest of the dead, which now appear

But things removed that hidden in thee lie!

Thou art the grave where buried love doth live,

Hung with the trophies of my lovers gone,

Who all their parts of me to thee did give;

That due of many now is thine alone:

Their images I loved I view in thee,

And thou, all they, hast all the all of me.

~ WS

31.

you're ore. gold. you were here before *homo*

sapiens dug you up and loved you. he

smelts you now for coin. immortal, you flee

from lover to lover; you cause revo-

lutions. you've borne the values of ancient

kings & serfs. you're the mother & the grave

of their longings & loves, the queen of trade:

once a rock, now the meaning of the earth.

i'm ether. your brother. once just some by-

product of primordial yeast, now i'm

man's symbol for 'the beyond', anaestha:

heaven, religion, values, morality.

some say we should be wed—i give you worth.

some force a choice—either ether or ore.

~ JD

XXXII.

If thou survive my well-contented day,

When that churl Death my bones with dust shall cover,

And shalt by fortune once more re-survey

These poor rude lines of thy deceased lover,

Compare them with the bettering of the time,

And though they be outstripp'd by every pen,

Reserve them for my love, not for their rhyme,

Exceeded by the height of happier men.

O, then vouchsafe me but this loving thought:

'Had my friend's Muse grown with this growing age,

A dearer birth than this his love had brought,

To march in ranks of better equipage:

But since he died and poets better prove,

Theirs for their style I'll read, his for his love.'

~ WS

32.

my not-ness: monotonous unravelling
of my sonnets; non-sets, not-*sens* settling

onto you like the loud hush of heavy snow; fall-
ing as silent as dust on grandma's old shawl,

and as efficient. feel my nothingness swell
again—just as before my birth—in battle

with my being. again *mei nemo* will win.
do i ask you to remember me? what mon-

ument will you raise to tracks that spoil virgin
fields of white? will you compare me to my sons?

each poet's death disentropies the world. sing,
if you want, when i dissolve. but know: nothing's

lost from my unshapely atoms...except green
math: some combo of 11 & 14.

~ JD

XXXIII.

Full many a glorious morning have I seen

Flatter the mountain-tops with sovereign eye,

Kissing with golden face the meadows green,

Gilding pale streams with heavenly alchemy;

Anon permit the basest clouds to ride

With ugly rack on his celestial face,

And from the forlorn world his visage hide,

Stealing unseen to west with this disgrace:

Even so my sun one early morn did shine

With all triumphant splendor on my brow;

But out, alack! he was but one hour mine;

The region cloud hath mask'd him from me now.

Yet him for this my love no whit disdaineth;

Suns of the world may stain when heaven's sun staineth.

~ WS

33.

Sunday: hail christ or helios: which dawn?

Tonic or gin? well / sick? which sets the tone.

Monday: 'reflection' means man's work is done on her

Supertonic: her strength—over-potions

Tuesday: two fight—sun / moon; man / woman

Mediant: mid-battle, choose a mood.

Wednesday: o-din of noon amid thy kin!

Subdominant: father serve son? O-men.

Thursday: philosophy's magic hammer

Dominant: thor—portent for apollo...

Friday's frigate, though, bears other news:

Superdominant queen of heaven laughs.

Saturday: then hearth, now field. chronos comes.

Leading tone: anticipate timeless return...

~ JD

XXXIV.

Why didst thou promise such a beauteous day,

And make me travel forth without my cloak,

To let base clouds o'ertake me in my way,

Hiding thy bravery in their rotten smoke?

'Tis not enough that through the cloud thou break,

To dry the rain on my storm-beaten face,

For no man well of such a salve can speak

That heals the wound and cures not the disgrace:

Nor can thy shame give physic to my grief;

Though thou repent, yet I have still the loss:

The offender's sorrow lends but weak relief

To him that bears the strong offence's cross.

Ah! but those tears are pearl which thy love sheds,

And they are rich and ransom all ill deeds.

34.

Twelve tribes, apostles, months, chromatic tones:

What, love, afraid your love's not so complete?

O swear not then sweet calm when thunder lulls.

SEVEN days, seals, trumpets, diatonic notes:

How do you give parched nomads fiery thoughts?

You tell them heaven's a resting-home for souls.

Ten lost tribes, metric runes, toes, fingers, feet:

Why should one decade trump the other ones,

Or thoughts return to twenties when they're gone?

Don't pretend to love me when I get old;

Or on Sundays; or when night sands on

Zephyrs & a bad hand of fireside pok-

Er subtract me softly from your harem's

Number. sing songs. make love. make yourself new.

~ JD

XXXV.

No more be grieved at that which thou hast done:

Roses have thorns, and silver fountains mud;

Clouds and eclipses stain both moon and sun,

And loathsome canker lives in sweetest bud.

All men make faults, and even I in this,

Authorizing thy trespass with compare,

Myself corrupting, salving thy amiss,

Excusing thy sins more than thy sins are;

For to thy sensual fault I bring in sense—

Thy adverse party is thy advocate—

And 'gainst myself a lawful plea commence:

Such civil war is in my love and hate

That I an accessory needs must be

To that sweet thief which sourly robs from me.

~ WS

35.

still a moment for your stillborn deeds, for
frenzied acts, my *hetero orgê*. *homo mensura*:
seize the dame. i, pluto: prosper by pome-
granates; pan: by theistic theo-rein,

-reign, -rain of hot. you bleed, spew from ripped limbs.
was madness my sad fate sent by bacchus?
no. but neither has this deity died.
instead, he's morphed. it's dawn. i yawn. i see,

recall this: i am he. "god's dead!"? against
this dogma: i am god. emit, omitter, time.
i commit this act, sublime. must you ask?
i hate you. mourn. you've left much undone.

and now i've disarmed you, black queen, venus.
i, mars, bring war. this move's my gauntlet. *check*.

~ JD

XXXVIII.

How can my Muse want subject to invent,

While thou dost breathe, that pour'st into my verse

Thine own sweet argument, too excellent

For every vulgar paper to rehearse?

O, give thyself the thanks, if aught in me

Worthy perusal stand against thy sight;

For who's so dumb that cannot write to thee,

When thou thyself dost give invention light?

Be thou the tenth Muse, ten times more in worth

Than those old nine which rhymers invocate;

And he that calls on thee, let him bring forth

Eternal numbers to outlive long date.

If my slight Muse do please these curious days,

The pain be mine, but thine shall be the praise.

~ WS

38.

in you i find my union with all things.

you're my dark portal into the sewers,

skyscrapers, and fierce mountaintops of being.

you germinate my distance and my hours.

i become your strange lava, the plasma

of your lightning, the cosmic showers you make

into my truth. when you summon the gods

and monsters of my subconscious like break-

ers of pounding surf, and play with my numb

appendages, somehow i still feel safe.

you make me fuck you and laugh at how dumb

we look...without bodies, sexed and unsexed

at once. you're my faith in the world, my *muse*—

my maker, my love, & my libido fused.

XXXIX.

O, how thy worth with manners may I sing,

When thou art all the better part of me?

What can mine own praise to mine own self bring?

And what is 't but mine own when I praise thee?

Even for this let us divided live,

And our dear love lose name of single one,

That by this separation I may give

That due to thee which thou deservest alone.

O absence, what a torment wouldst thou prove,

Were it not thy sour leisure gave sweet leave

To entertain the time with thoughts of love,

Which time and thoughts so sweetly doth deceive,

And that thou teachest how to make one twain,

By praising him here who doth hence remain!

~ WS

39.

when, love, we make these vows, what do we mean:

"i'm yours; you're mine"? what kind of union do

they bring? sometimes an outward bond: a bead

of glue, some nails, a prison for the will.

sometimes a living tie—the fibers of

our souls enmeshed. and almost always: both.

we wove propriety into our love—

and now possession's got the best of us.

so go. though we both dread our cargo may

be lost, washed up dead on some sandy shore,

driving our psycho-financiers crazy.

or...(god forbid)...some other should borrow

my chattel and return it unmaligned....

well then, *adieu*... ...i love you, too... ...*you're mine*.

~ JD

XL.

Take all my loves, my love, yea, take them all;

What hast thou then more than thou hadst before?

No love, my love, that thou mayst true love call;

All mine was thine before thou hadst this more.

Then if for my love thou my love receivest,

I cannot blame thee for my love thou usest;

But yet be blamed, if thou thyself deceivest

By wilful taste of what thyself refusest.

I do forgive thy robbery, gentle thief,

Although thou steal thee all my poverty;

And yet, love knows, it is a greater grief

To bear love's wrong than hate's known injury.

Lascivious grace, in whom all ill well shows,

Kill me with spites; yet we must not be foes.

~ WS

40.

all headings of my life, my love, my vows

are meaningless unless my will is free.

i seek no prize but what my head allows.

and where my head goes, there my heart will be.

so take my heart, indeed, so take my head—

my head, my love, gives us its full resign.

while drunken passions lure us to this bed,

our minds consort (our consorts need not mind).

slaves to a reason that enslaves us all,

a fiery lust inflames my tongue, your lips.

by conscious choice united, we both feel

the gentleness of true companionship.

you might forget the tender words i said,

but don't forget: i gave both heart and head.

~ JD

XLI.

Those petty wrongs that liberty commits,

When I am sometime absent from thy heart,

Thy beauty and thy years full well befits,

For still temptation follows where thou art.

Gentle thou art and therefore to be won,

Beauteous thou art, therefore to be assailed;

And when a woman woos, what woman's son

Will sourly leave her till she have prevailed?

Ay me! but yet thou mightest my seat forbear,

And chide thy beauty and thy straying youth,

Who lead thee in their riot even there

Where thou art forced to break a twofold truth,

Hers by thy beauty tempting her to thee,

Thine, by thy beauty being false to me.

~ WS

41.

your virtue's vicious circle orbits me.

your urges never look me in the face.

i love your being who you want to be—

the cage alone will make the tigress pace.

the liberty to be yourself is yours.

the suicidal earth would strike the sun

if center-seeking was the only force.

without centrifugal, two melt to one.

but "two" means truth grows out of covered lies;

but "two" means codependent opposites;

for part of you to live, part of me dies;

you make withdrawals from me your deposits.

my partner in the dark, i wake to you.

we are the lies that make each other true.

~ JD

XLII.

That thou hast her, it is not all my grief,

And yet it may be said I loved her dearly;

That she hath thee, is of my wailing chief,

A loss in love that touches me more nearly.

Loving offenders, thus I will excuse ye:

Thou dost love her, because thou knowst I love her;

And for my sake even so doth she abuse me,

Suffering my friend for my sake to approve her.

If I lose thee, my loss is my love's gain,

And losing her, my friend hath found that loss;

Both find each other, and I lose both twain,

And both for my sake lay on me this cross:

But here's the joy; my friend and I are one;

Sweet flattery! then she loves but me alone.

~ WS

42.

you thaw to me, like a first frost on ripe

grapes thaws to the sun. and like grapes you and

i have fermented separately, now snipped

and crushed together in this wet moment.

i didn't know ecstasy until your

silky-clean, full-bodied, firm tannin-drip

washed over me. my essence drifts on our

blent juice. our fluids make new wine. i sip

your pure, moist night-love. poured together, with

earth and autumn-air as witnesses, we

mingle with many drops, flowing past myths

of propriety, of monogamy.

still, my memory savors your long finish.

like blood & water, aftertastes replenish.

~ JD

XLIII.

When most I wink, then do mine eyes best see,

For all the day they view things unrespected;

But when I sleep, in dreams they look on thee,

And darkly bright are bright in dark directed.

Then thou, whose shadow shadows doth make bright,

How would thy shadow's form form happy show

To the clear day with thy much clearer light,

When to unseeing eyes thy shade shines so!

How would, I say, mine eyes be blessed made

By looking on thee in the living day,

When in dead night thy fair imperfect shade

Through heavy sleep on sightless eyes doth stay!

All days are nights to see till I see thee,

And nights bright days when dreams do show thee me.

~ WS

43.

i met your eyes, i thought, i met your mind:

eyes—quick, elusive, bright—like flashing swords;

your long lashes enslaved me; lids like rinds

of watermelons; pupils ripe with words.

i coyly keep the mental polaroid

i took of you (the image is the thing).

when i dream of you, i try to avoid

thinking of what i took, of what i'm taking....

...truth is, i've always worshipped images...

(they unify my life, my dreams, my past—

i can't remember without replicas)

...for they worship me. i'm king of my thoughts.

i rule all that i gaze, all i compose—

the mind rules images when eyelids close.

~ JD

XLIV.

If the dull substance of my flesh were thought,

Injurious distance should not stop my way;

For then despite of space I would be brought,

From limits far remote where thou dost stay.

No matter then although my foot did stand

Upon the farthest earth removed from thee;

For nimble thought can jump both sea and land

As soon as think the place where he would be.

But ah! thought kills me that I am not thought,

To leap large lengths of miles when thou art gone,

But that so much of earth and water wrought

I must attend time's leisure with my moan,

Receiving nought by elements so slow

But heavy tears, badges of either's woe.

~ WS

44.

two witnesses—the spirit and the blood—

these two are one. my body's not a *fab-*

ula rasa. embodied in your thought,

each thing i touch tells me not just of ob-

jects, but of you. you've always impressed me,

like golden rings impress the soft, wry wax

with their hard laughter. your thought is hard, my

body soft. my hard thought, hard love, hard facts

too, penetrate your soft flesh. my truth, my

love, my needs inform you. caress me—your

own body of thought, body of love. flesh

out your thought in me. then you'll know why

my eyes have smile-lines when i'm 84,

why my wrinkled skin is your only wish.

~ JD

III

XLV.

The other two, slight air and purging fire,

Are both with thee, wherever I abide;

The first my thought, the other my desire,

These present-absent with swift motion slide.

For when these quicker elements are gone

In tender embassy of love to thee,

My life, being made of four, with two alone

Sinks down to death, oppress'd with melancholy;

Until life's composition be recured

By those swift messengers return'd from thee,

Who even but now come back again, assured

Of thy fair health, recounting it to me:

This told, I joy; but then no longer glad,

I send them back again and straight grow sad.

~ WS

45.

truth and water, too, grip her sighing life. I

who bathe wet reverie, *i* bathe her id,

tether thought & memory, shift desire: thy

wet amnesio-births fit thee, wild sonnet-steps!

oceans felt her meek requesting nowhere.

tested before heavenly motions,

i endure hematology: a fine, fit womb-flow...

and happy, smoothest, well-worn, dishonest dick.

i coursed omnipresence, but to fill

wet truth-beds i forget—memory freshens *sens*

but back-anagrams *ennui*, whose code wove

truth (or lie) into each thing of my fate.

in day, old truth-jobs tell ego nothing...

...as backward night-songs edit & anagram the id.

~ JD

XLVI.

Mine eye and heart are at a mortal war

How to divide the conquest of thy sight;

Mine eye my heart thy picture's sight would bar,

My heart mine eye the freedom of that right.

My heart doth plead that thou in him dost lie —

A closet never pierced with crystal eyes —

But the defendant doth that plea deny

And says in him thy fair appearance lies.

To 'cide this title is impanneled

A quest of thoughts, all tenants to the heart,

And by their verdict is determined

The clear eye's moiety and the dear heart's part:

As thus; mine eye's due is thy outward part,

And my heart's right thy inward love of heart.

~ WS

46.

a blind girl and a paralyzed boy are
fighting over a toy. the blind girl wants
to feel its movement in her heart's dim night;
the other simply wants to gaze—perhaps
its form could melt his still eyes' frozen sight.

my heart is blind. my eye is numb. you are the toy.
my id reminds. my ego plumbs. a girl. a boy.

does desire dwell in time?

heart teases & seduces gaze by promising desire;
habituates perception with her groping pleasure-fire.

meanwhile my eyes appear to be
the owners of all they see
(storehoused in memory),
conquistadors for an eyeless lust
that's useless to eyes' "–ologies"...

...for how could love & wisdom touch?

~ JD

XLVII.

Betwixt mine eye and heart a league is took,

And each doth good turns now unto the other:

When that mine eye is famish'd for a look,

Or heart in love with sighs himself doth smother,

With my love's picture then my eye doth feast

And to the painted banquet bids my heart;

Another time mine eye is my heart's guest

And in his thoughts of love doth share a part:

So, either by thy picture or my love,

Thyself away art present still with me;

For thou not farther than my thoughts canst move,

And I am still with them and they with thee;

Or, if they sleep, thy picture in my sight

Awakes my heart to heart's and eye's delight.

~ WS

47.

can we philosophize? i love you. i

try to love your body, but your body

keeps me far from you in this agony

we call space. so i love your heart, your mind,

your will, your life, your "chi" —all that makes you

who you want to be. here we mingle. here

heart knows heart & mind loves mind. it's here our

souls commune. souls make love, not bodies. do

bodies touch? a mere juxtaposition

without love's knowing verdict. otherwise,

you're just another object for my eyes.

in answer to this desperate condition,

mind transfers love to bodies that i see:

and makes love, science, and philosophy...

~ JD

XLVIII.

How careful was I, when I took my way,

Each trifle under truest bars to thrust,

That to my use it might unused stay

From hands of falsehood, in sure wards of trust!

But thou, to whom my jewels trifles are,

Most worthy of comfort, now my greatest grief,

Thou, best of dearest and mine only care,

Art left the prey of every vulgar thief.

Thee have I not lock'd up in any chest,

Save where thou art not, though I feel thou art,

Within the gentle closure of my breast,

From whence at pleasure thou mayst come and part;

And even thence thou wilt be stol'n, I fear,

For truth proves thievish for a prize so dear.

~ WS

48.

...or so they say. but our love knows better.

consumus ergo cogitamus. we

dwell in our love. here we know as we are

known. and though my feet have wandered, weary

& smeared with earth, far from your hearth—

my being still stays with you, my homeland.

my *terra incognita,* i don't fear

your cartographers. i know your sands and

oceans. who could catch your zephyrs as they

caress your sloping hills, ripe with golden

wheat-harvests? who dares climb your fertile grape-

vines or taste your thick, sweet honeycombs? then

let them bring their coordinates, diagrams

& grids to this land where i are & you am.

XLIX.

Against that time, if ever that time come,

When I shall see thee frown on my defects,

When as thy love hath cast his utmost sum,

Call'd to that audit by advised respects;

Against that time when thou shalt strangely pass

And scarcely greet me with that sun thine eye,

When love, converted from the thing it was,

Shall reasons find of settled gravity,—

Against that time do I ensconce me here

Within the knowledge of mine own desert,

And this my hand against myself uprear,

To guard the lawful reasons on thy part:

To leave poor me thou hast the strength of laws,

Since why to love I can allege no cause.

~ WS

49.

Against that Time, if it should chance to come,

When summoned to account for all my Acts,

When lumping all my Projects to a sum,

Your Audit sues me and reclaims them back;

Against that Time, when you return to me

And ask me how I've lived this borrowed Life,

When Love, converted from its apathy,

Finds sudden cause for Acts, desperate & rife,—

Against that Time, I'll hide myself in Tasks,

Concede my Guilt, & make sunshiny hay;

I'll execute my Sentence, if you ask—

Since it was going to happen anyway.

My Being, it's your right to ruin me,

Since I've been squandering your Treasury.

~ JD

L.

How heavy do I journey on the way,

When what I seek, my weary travel's end,

Doth teach that ease and that repose to say

'Thus far the miles are measured from thy friend!'

The beast that bears me, tired with my woe,

Plods dully on, to bear that weight in me,

As if by some instinct the wretch did know

His rider loved not speed, being made from thee:

The bloody spur cannot provoke him on

That sometimes anger thrusts into his hide;

Which heavily he answers with a groan,

More sharp to me than spurring to his side;

For that same groan doth put this in my mind;

My grief lies onward and my joy behind.

~ WS

50.

I bear your fears, your tears, your late *adieu*;

and in departing, I must trust this dyn-

amis to bring me to return and to

your arms. This stubborn war engine of mine,

this odd corporeal carriage, bears me

away—(my only fellows now: the ver-

dant fields, and vivid upright shadows set

ablaze with gold and red)—my cycling tread

keeps laying down its small circumference.

So I, remiss, this missive send to sol-

ace, fingering your strings of soul, while my

soul, motoring between God and devil,

imp and angel, erupts, reborn and rent—

bare, livid—each new lonely moment.

~ JD

LI.

Thus can my love excuse the slow offence
Of my dull bearer when from thee I speed:
From where thou art why should I haste me thence?
Till I return, of posting is no need.

O, what excuse will my poor beast then find,
When swift extremity can seem but slow?
Then should I spur, though mounted on the wind;
In winged speed no motion shall I know:

Then can no horse with my desire keep pace;
Therefore desire of perfect'st love being made,
Shall neigh—no dull flesh—in his fiery race;
But love, for love, thus shall excuse my jade;

Since from thee going he went wilful-slow,
Towards thee I'll run, and give him leave to go.

~ WS

51.

our truth lies here & there & everywhere:

we play upon its rain-soaked, muddy grounds,

this grassy plain of unmarked graves (profound?

we splatter up the muck of our forbears.)

why is it, then, that when we're not at sport,

when you and i go to respective homes,

you keep my truth, and torn from you I roam,

a truthless vagrant, desolate *tout-court*?

my zen-rise, bright & dripping, from the sea

is dumb without you. deprived of earth-names,

swollen with sun's travail, i burst to flames:

his steeds of language are too hot for me.

so headlong now, i fly toward my demise,

twice mute: unworded by both earth & skies.

~ JD

LII.

So am I as the rich, whose blessed key

Can bring him to his sweet up-locked treasure,

The which he will not every hour survey,

For blunting the fine point of seldom pleasure.

Therefore are feasts so solemn and so rare,

Since, seldom coming, in the long year set,

Like stones of worth they thinly placed are,

Or captain jewels in the carcanet.

So is the time that keeps you as my chest,

Or as the wardrobe which the robe doth hide,

To make some special instant special blest,

By new unfolding his imprison'd pride.

Blessed are you, whose worthiness gives scope,

Being had, to triumph, being lack'd, to hope.

~ WS

52.

1, 2, 3... numbering gives possessive

adjectives. I *count* you "Mine." I place these

handy tags on being, weeks, suits, wombs, lives,

coins, words, days, works—all that enlarges Me.

"inside," "enclosure"...this I also need

(without it all My goods might fly away).

locked-up in number, Mine: now let men read

of My accounts, secure for Their assay.

your "in" is not like Mine—I bank on it.

your generous 'in' gives interest to My greed.

I make your vessel grounds My vassalettes,

your ovum's just the oven for My bread.

I seize into My stores your giving-"in"—

ἐν τοι, ἐν μου I *have* all that I *am*.

~ JD

LIII.

What is your substance, whereof are you made,

That millions of strange shadows on you tend?

Since every one hath, every one, one shade,

And you, but one, can every shadow lend.

Describe Adonis, and the counterfeit

Is poorly imitated after you;

On Helen's cheek all art of beauty set,

And you in Grecian tires are painted new:

Speak of the spring and foison of the year;

The one doth shadow of your beauty show,

The other as your bounty doth appear;

And you in every blessed shape we know.

In all external grace you have some part,

But you like none, none you, for constant heart.

~ WS

53.

quid tua substantia, fabrica?
creator-lord of untold shadow-hosts,
you, everywhere & nowhere, like the sun,
make all your bright guests into your dark ghosts.

prometheus' theft pales to your greed:
all things exchange for your consuming fire.
in proteus, your ever-shifting need
reveals its shape & substance as desire.

as summer brings its scorching light & heat,
your fires use all whose labor uses you.
winter's the symbol, cold & desolate,
of what your unseen, icy hand can do.

each good & value lives in your fine shade...
including us: traded for what we trade.

~ JD

LIV.

O, how much more doth beauty beauteous seem

By that sweet ornament which truth doth give!

The rose looks fair, but fairer we it deem

For that sweet odour which doth in it live.

The canker-blooms have full as deep a dye

As the perfumed tincture of the roses,

Hang on such thorns and play as wantonly

When summer's breath their masked buds discloses:

But, for their virtue only is their show,

They live unwoo'd and unrespected fade,

Die to themselves. Sweet roses do not so;

Of their sweet deaths are sweetest odours made:

And so of you, beauteous and lovely youth,

When that shall fade, my verse distills your truth.

~ WS

54.

rose-boughs mature anew sweet, dubious dreams.

mind-candy-flora blends its nutritive

aromas. their hooks snare us (deities,

words): and we show thorn-prints definitive.

thus strangled, truth has lulled asleep our eyes,

and once presumed dead, winks. ormus composes

pangs, allah mourns, as they grant some money

& others death, where grass-bent mud disposes.

sun-warmed air flirts. dews, rosy with airflows,

play in untrue glands. undetected they

fly. truth gets heavy. noses, fooled, follow,

unwary. dead-god weed-smells float away.

sad rose of truth, true love, as honeyed dews,

blend accolades, lies merged with shimmered truths.

~ JD

LV.

Not marble, nor the gilded monuments

Of princes, shall outlive this powerful rhyme;

But you shall shine more bright in these contents

Than unswept stone besmear'd with sluttish time.

When wasteful war shall statues overturn,

And broils root out the work of masonry,

Nor Mars his sword nor war's quick fire shall burn

The living record of your memory.

'Gainst death and all-oblivious enmity

Shall you pace forth; your praise shall still find room

Even in the eyes of all posterity

That wear this world out to the ending doom.

So, till the judgment that yourself arise,

You live in this, and dwell in lover's eyes.

~ WS

55.

...dark oneiric anamnesis calls...

time slows for us

as we step through

into eternity

and like a grand reversal

our faces feel compressed

as though we're swung in cosmic centrifuge

before eye sees

our bodies feel

their morph of sentient clay remold

and caught up in the resurrection-swirl of humanity

we stand before Him

new bodies bend involuntarily at knee that Day

without choice mankind is cleft

faceless

all the colors and flavors of our lives become

the candy-stripe and swirl

on a grain of sand

too late

now that

The Day of the LORD is at hand.

~ JD

LVI.

Sweet love, renew thy force; be it not said

Thy edge should blunter be than appetite,

Which but to-day by feeding is allay'd,

To-morrow sharpen'd in his former might:

So, love, be thou; although to-day thou fill

Thy hungry eyes even till they wink with fullness,

To-morrow see again, and do not kill

The spirit of love with a perpetual dullness.

Let this sad interim like the ocean be

Which parts the shore, where two contracted new

Come daily to the banks, that, when they see

Return of love, more blest may be the view;

Else call it winter, which being full of care

Makes summer's welcome thrice more wish'd, more rare.

~ WS

56.

i soared. eye-sored, i (sword, ice or dice), sort

dilemmas for the strife that pulls apart

here from there, now from then, me from you, words

from letters, her from him.... problems like why

i used to fly, but now am bound to ar-

bitrate; used to play, but now, like a gray

judge, sit here solemnly. WAR, WINTER, FATE:

what kinds of things am I supposed to solve?

WAR, WINTER, FATE: why emulate me? or

what would come if you could pantomime

primordial strife, primordial love?

strive against the strife that built this sea of

pain between you, built your love? *love* this strife?

WAR, WINTER, FATE: accuse / excuse your life.

~ JD

LVII.

Being your slave, what should I do but tend
Upon the hours and times of your desire?
I have no precious time at all to spend,
Nor services to do, till you require.

Nor dare I chide the world-without-end hour
Whilst I, my sovereign, watch the clock for you,
Nor think the bitterness of absence sour
When you have bid your servant once adieu;

Nor dare I question with my jealous thought
Where you may be, or your affairs suppose,
But, like a sad slave, stay and think of nought
Save, where you are how happy you make those.

So true a fool is love that in your will,
Though you do any thing, he thinks no ill.

~ WS

57.

take me, your own love slave. have me. *also,*

ich habe hunger. ho sete. ...you have

your drives, so have your way with me. although

you have your being, life, & time...who gave

you what you're taking? what do you *have*? a

memorial stockpile of "images"? the

"woof" of some ideal "conceptual grid"?

and how do you have this *having*? is it

yours? "inside" you? counted? controlled or free?

this *having* hides & manifests your world:

you-and-your-surroundings—your furniture

& food; cars, gadgets, friends (perhaps me, too)—

your ever-shifting, strange self-recipe.

have me: let me surround / belong-with you.

~ JD

LVIII.

That god forbid that made me first your slave,

I should in thought control your times of pleasure,

Or at your hand the account of hours to crave,

Being your vassal, bound to stay your leisure!

O, let me suffer, being at your beck,

The imprison'd absence of your liberty;

And patience, tame to sufferance, bide each cheque,

Without accusing you of injury.

Be where you list, your charter is so strong

That you yourself may privilege your time

To what you will; to you it doth belong

Yourself to pardon of self-doing crime.

I am to wait, though waiting so be hell;

Not blame your pleasure, be it ill or well.

~ WS

58.

whatever victimizing super-ego

made me your bitch won't even let me use

telepathy to control your orgasms

or remote-viewing to watch over you!

i live in my sadomasochistic,

quixotic dream-cosmos where love means control,

where my mind feels real pain when it stabs

itself with the dream-blades of your freedom.

i'm pissed because my fancied banns don't give

you claustrophobia. but i'm so whipped,

i'd love you no matter what you did, since

i'm insecure & feel unworthy of you.

so since i can't keep you from having fun,

i'll give you my half-hearted permission.

~ JD

LIX.

If there be nothing new, but that which is

Hath been before, how are our brains beguiled,

Which, labouring for invention, bear amiss

The second burden of a former child!

O, that record could with a backward look,

Even of five hundred courses of the sun,

Show me your image in some antique book,

Since mind at first in character was done!

That I might see what the old world could say

To this composed wonder of your frame;

Whether we are mended, or whether better they,

Or whether revolution be the same.

O, sure I am, the wits of former days

To subjects worse have given admiring praise.

~ WS

59.

if nothing's new beneath this burning star,

this turning eye, why try to be unique

or why strive to bend earth's orbit to our

rectilinear notion of history?

this race of mother earth forgets its birth

(though mother wove herself into the child,

inscribed her values on us blocks of earth,

& styling thus our pleasure-centers, smiled.)

in main, our frame's hard-wired to reproduce

and be forgotten: we're circuits in her

sempiternal flow. but our minds seduce

us, writhe, and try to write our tale with per-

manent ink: like endless life through bard-rhymes,

or saving our neurons to a hard-drive.

~ JD

LX.

Like as the waves make towards the pebbled shore,

So do our minutes hasten to their end;

Each changing place with that which goes before,

In sequent toil all forwards do contend.

Nativity, once in the main of light,

Crawls to maturity, wherewith being crown'd,

Crooked eclipses 'gainst his glory fight,

And Time that gave doth now his gift confound.

Time doth transfix the flourish set on youth

And delves the parallels in beauty's brow,

Feeds on the rarities of nature's truth,

And nothing stands but for his scythe to mow:

And yet to times in hope my verse shall stand,

Praising thy worth, despite his cruel hand.

~ WS

60.

the deep blue groundswells heave & sigh. oceans

mount & drop, upsurge & falter, crest & crush,

convulse, disperse in foam. always motion

but no coasts, no ghosts, only bodies of

water, eyes of fire, moonlit vaults, and songs

of flotsam whales. and it's an art to feel

these bodies ours, to own them and belong.

although each corpse must plunge, succumb, and keel

at some uncertain hour, we're legion and

our incarnations vast. our salt is in

the seas, our torso in the trees: human

life worn by wood, by steel, by rose, by ink.

in all our bodies, subtle, sentient:

in you and in these words, spending and spent.

~ JD

LXI.

Is it thy will thy image should keep open
My heavy eyelids to the weary night?
Dost thou desire my slumbers should be broken,
While shadows like to thee do mock my sight?

Is it thy spirit that thou send'st from thee
So far from home into my deeds to pry,
To find out shames and idle hours in me,
The scope and tenor of thy jealousy?

O, no! thy love, though much, is not so great:
It is my love that keeps mine eye awake;
Mine own true love that doth my rest defeat,
To play the watchman ever for thy sake:

For thee watch I whilst thou dost wake elsewhere,
From me far off, with others all too near.

~ WS

61.

when drowsy thoughts like dew condense on you
and memories somnambulate with dreams
as the montage of fantasy and truth
mutates and shifts like shadows and moonbeams,

when i imagine that your astral ghost
is rustling through my mental leaves, stirring
my joys and conscience, recalling our lost
time together, soft as a stream's babbling,

then smiling, i imbibe this balm of love,
and feel again the ardor of your toes,
and the smell of your hair, and the heft of
your curved torso, and the stroke of your nose,

and in this bliss, this bacchan *déjà vu*,
i'm transubstantiated into you.

~ JD

LXII.

Sin of self-love possesseth all mine eye

And all my soul and all my every part;

And for this sin there is no remedy,

It is so grounded inward in my heart.

Methinks no face so gracious is as mine,

No shape so true, no truth of such account;

And for myself mine own worth do define,

As I all other in all worths surmount.

But when my glass shows me myself indeed,

Beated and chopp'd with tann'd antiquity,

Mine own self-love quite contrary I read;

Self so self-loving were iniquity.

'Tis thee, my self, that for myself I praise,

Painting my age with beauty of thy days.

~ WS

62.

self-ish in every body i've become

self-less as my whole world mutates into

self-like artifacts & folks: *mutandum*

for all i touch, a boundless retinue.

since all the world's a mirror for my *sein*

& i'm a mirror, too, for all i meet,

we janus-faced, odd specula align,

a mobile host of carbon parodies.

oh self, flesh of my flesh, bone of my bone,

like narcissus, i love myself in you.

i'm sad, i'm midas, miser of my own,

bankrupt midst my beloved revenue.

imperial, golden worlds attire me—

a boundless self self-loving boundlessly.

~ JD

LXIII.

Against my love shall be, as I am now,

With Time's injurious hand crush'd and o'er-worn;

When hours have drain'd his blood and fill'd his brow

With lines and wrinkles; when his youthful morn

Hath travell'd on to age's steepy night,

And all those beauties whereof now he's king

Are vanishing or vanish'd out of sight,

Stealing away the treasure of his spring;

For such a time do I now fortify

Against confounding age's cruel knife,

That he shall never cut from memory

My sweet love's beauty, though my lover's life:

His beauty shall in these black lines be seen,

And they shall live, and he in them still green.

~ WS

63.

the *now* of how i feel does not depend

on days & hours, but on some secret syn-

tax of triggers & transferences which

minutes do not measure, some symphony

whose codas & caesuras compose this

morphing mindscape of my moods, wants, & needs.

perhaps i feel this way because i've worked

my job too long, or lived with you these years,

or had a coffee with my breakfast or

because this morning's smells refresh old fears

of failure. at any rate, my now is

now, and i feel my pulse, like a foregone

conclusion, beating in my center-mass

as in some inchoate automaton.

~ JD

LXIV.

When I have seen by Time's fell hand defaced

The rich proud cost of outworn buried age;

When sometime lofty towers I see down-razed

And brass eternal slave to mortal rage;

When I have seen the hungry ocean gain

Advantage on the kingdom of the shore,

And the firm soil win of the watery main,

Increasing store with loss and loss with store;

When I have seen such interchange of state,

Or state itself confounded to decay;

Ruin hath taught me thus to ruminate,

That Time will come and take my love away.

This thought is as a death, which cannot choose

But weep to have that which it fears to lose.

~ WS

64.

The ancient slab is loosened from the wall;
it thunders dusty haze as clash of swords
resounds the barded strife of bygone lords—
though all seems silent as Rome's ruins fall.

A-trouncing trumpets summon trumping-chords
as swelling Bar-bar scores dispel the dreams
of perpetuity. Aged culture-seams
in silence shred today before mute-words

of upward-ambling smoke. It dissipates
and mocks as though the tired relics knew
they fled helpless historians into
vague nostalgia. The dust now settling waits

for dusk to meet horizon...forlorn again
in its joy to start anew another paean.

~ JD

LXV.

Since brass, nor stone, nor earth, nor boundless sea,

But sad mortality o'er-sways their power,

How with this rage shall beauty hold a plea,

Whose action is no stronger than a flower?

O, how shall summer's honey breath hold out

Against the wreckful siege of battering days,

When rocks impregnable are not so stout,

Nor gates of steel so strong, but Time decays?

O fearful meditation! where, alack,

Shall Time's best jewel from Time's chest lie hid?

Or what strong hand can hold his swift foot back?

Or who his spoil of beauty can forbid?

O, none, unless this miracle have might,

That in black ink my love may still shine bright.

~ WS

65.

since "stabbed," or "hanged," or "drowned," or "overdosed"

or countless other acts are titled, "death,"

and "hot," "attractive," "pretty" & a host

of others we tag "beauty," in one breath,

as on a battlefield, two equals meet.

this clash of titan signifiers sways

our value-laden human hearts whose beat

drowns out earth's laughter at our shadow-plays.

with "death" and "beauty" locked in mortal strife,

we genome-bearers procreate & die.

the gene-codes we've affixed to beauty's life

are letter-combos made to be untied

by our words. so like nice language-bearers,

let's transmit "beauty" & "death" to our heirs.

~ JD

LXVI.

Tired with all these, for restful death I cry,

As, to behold desert a beggar born,

And needy nothing trimm'd in jollity,

And purest faith unhappily forsworn,

And guilded honour shamefully misplaced,

And maiden virtue rudely strumpeted,

And right perfection wrongfully disgraced,

And strength by limping sway disabled,

And art made tongue-tied by authority,

And folly doctor-like controlling skill,

And simple truth miscall'd simplicity,

And captive good attending captain ill:

Tired with all these, from these would I be gone,

Save that, to die, I leave my love alone.

~ WS

66.

trapped in this web of names, for choice i yearn,

as i have seen the pope turn atheist,

& maudlin whores dubbed saints while sinners burn,

& native grain by foreign hand turned grist,

& poverty called profit, INC.,

& war named entertainment by the press,

& colored skin stripped of humanity,

& gender made a reason to oppress,

& science pressed to serve atomic bombs,

& killers sentenced to their liberty,

& local business killed by world.com,

& families rent by ideology,

trapped in this web of names, for choice i cry,

consuming & consumed-by what i buy.

~ JD

IV

LXVII.

Ah! wherefore with infection should he live,

And with his presence grace impiety,

That sin by him advantage should achieve

And lace itself with his society?

Why should false painting imitate his cheek

And steal dead seeing of his living hue?

Why should poor beauty indirectly seek

Roses of shadow, since his rose is true?

Why should he live, now Nature bankrupt is,

Beggar'd of blood to blush through lively veins?

For she hath no exchequer now but his,

And, proud of many, lives upon his gains.

O, him she stores, to show what wealth she had

In days long since, before these last so bad.

~ WS

67.

how do we humans treat the earth?
we buy and sell her land.
this helps us multiply our wealth,
"supply must meet demand."

propriety's our battle-cry,
as we defy the foe
of wind & weather, earth & sky,
to reap more than we sow.

we occupy earth's neutral mounds.
our unseen fingers try
to wrestle secrets from her grounds.
we pry & quantify

& price her gems, relying on
her waters, oils, & ores.
our science shatters her protons
& squanders gaia's stores.

so what will be our alibi
when godlike earth draws nigh
and asks us why we gratify
our lusts with her supply?

~ JD

LXVIII.

Thus is his cheek the map of days outworn,

When beauty lived and died as flowers do now,

Before the bastard signs of fair were born,

Or durst inhabit on a living brow;

Before the golden tresses of the dead,

The right of sepulchres, were shorn away,

To live a second life on second head;

Ere beauty's dead fleece made another gay:

In him those holy antique hours are seen,

Without all ornament, itself and true,

Making no summer of another's green,

Robbing no old to dress his beauty new;

And him as for a map doth Nature store,

To show false Art what beauty was of yore.

~ WS

68.

we wear our wigs and usually forget

that our ideals of "beauty" are just fads

that we inherit—hairs and value-sets

which grew in heads now fashionably dead.

of course, it's false & fleeting mimicry

that wigs make humans into apes. but where

do "righteousness" & "justice" sprout? are we

not wigs here too, dead people's heirs? we bear

these cults of superficiality

whose verdicts / fashion statements / sentences

seep mercury into our wants & needs—

we mammal-hordes swell to our cults' defenses.

was some lost state of nature value-shorn,

before such bastard signs of "fair" were born?

~ JD

LXIX.

Those parts of thee that the world's eye doth view

Want nothing that the thought of hearts can mend;

All tongues, the voice of souls, give thee that due,

Uttering bare truth, even so as foes commend.

Thy outward thus with outward praise is crown'd;

But those same tongues that give thee so thine own

In other accents do this praise confound

By seeing farther than the eye hath shown.

They look into the beauty of thy mind,

And that, in guess, they measure by thy deeds;

Then, churls, their thoughts, although their eyes were kind,

To thy fair flower add the rank smell of weeds:

But why thy odour matcheth not thy show,

The solve is this, that thou dost common grow.

~ WS

69.

our words commune and, in their surplus, feed

each other meanings toward a common end.

one word's supply fulfills another's need—

syntagms straighten, polysemies bend.

a proper name, like property, insures

identity—an essence, self-contained,

with fixed, inherent properties. since force

& action forge our selves, we might begin

to think about ourselves as proper verbs:

"things *are*" becomes "things *thing*;" "i *am*" begets

"i *i*." but at what price would we preserve

uniqueness? a world of lonely monads.

aloof & smug, *bourgeois*, we egos walk

as proper names through common lands of talk.

~ JD

LXX.

That thou art blamed shall not be thy defect,

For slander's mark was ever yet the fair;

The ornament of beauty is suspect,

A crow that flies in heaven's sweetest air.

So thou be good, slander doth but approve

Thy worth the greater, being woo'd of time;

For canker vice the sweetest buds doth love,

And thou present'st a pure unstained prime.

Thou hast pass'd by the ambush of young days,

Either not assail'd or victor being charged;

Yet this thy praise cannot be so thy praise,

To tie up envy evermore enlarged:

If some suspect of ill mask'd not thy show,

Then thou alone kingdoms of hearts shouldst owe.

~ WS

70.

you don't want fame or a great name, do you?

a good name will suffice. you want people

to like you. you want to be likable,

but you still want to feel like you can do

whatever you want. sure, you've had your share

of "edgy" moves & calculated risks.

so you're seen as a leader, like a fisc-

al genius who blunders under radar

but whose portfolio always rises.

you pay your taxes, buy new things, and greet

people politely. you watch movies, but

you smoke. what should i tell you? are you wise?

at least you're prudent. you chase your dreams while

driving the speed limit. are you beautiful?

LXXI.

No longer mourn for me when I am dead

Than you shall hear the surly sullen bell

Give warning to the world that I am fled

From this vile world, with vilest worms to dwell:

Nay, if you read this line, remember not

The hand that writ it; for I love you so

That I in your sweet thoughts would be forgot

If thinking on me then should make you woe.

O, if, I say, you look upon this verse

When I perhaps compounded am with clay,

Do not so much as my poor name rehearse.

But let your love even with my life decay,

Lest the wise world should look into your moan

And mock you with me after I am gone.

~ WS

71.

let us go then, You and I, and add an-

other Faggot to the pyre. let's burn our

Niggard Will, Mind, Consciousness—all the banns

that bind Us to this dark, unspeaking hour.

the You is mother of the I, the I

has fathered It. this Trinity is styled,

We muse, tattooed to Being's face—hereby

We tag each tired speck of Truth & Guile.

I sweep my metaphors into a pile...

(like crab-grass or the brambles overhead—

this thorny web of words, our domicile—

a gnarled thicket, tangled, black and dead.)

...transfix them to the blaze and clear the sky—

i am my libido...and yet, not "I"...

~ JD

LXXII.

O, lest the world should task you to recite

What merit lived in me, that you should love

After my death, dear love, forget me quite,

For you in me can nothing worthy prove;

Unless you would devise some virtuous lie,

To do more for me than mine own desert,

And hang more praise upon deceased I

Than niggard truth would willingly impart:

O, lest your true love may seem false in this,

That you for love speak well of me untrue,

My name be buried where my body is,

And live no more to shame nor me nor you.

For I am shamed by that which I bring forth,

And so should you, to love things nothing worth.

~ WS

72.

dreams number us like pi. runes shift. nights rewind

daytime pleasure-piles. dream-looms create our id.

moods shift. words deviate. needs brew. pleasures rise.

time slows. too late? wait! foreign minds live in

us! quick-minds, free-minds, minds-we-never-mind,

unknown, gyrate! neuro-rhymes measure our

minds, *for our minds rhyme.* crude ego-emanations

distort nodes. id, (whose basic neuro-spacetime rhymes),

plays its tune. space drones before fate unites

dreams' lore to unsung measures. whole dimensions

gyrate. new number-games donate quick minds &

weave through fate's loom. fears, hopes, digits, or devils

collide here—labor stored in gold-mines, lives, lightcone-

piles. fate loops through dreams & pleasure-looms....

~ JD

LXXIII.

That time of year thou mayst in me behold

When yellow leaves, or none, or few, do hang

Upon those boughs which shake against the cold,

Bare ruin'd choirs, where late the sweet birds sang.

In me thou seest the twilight of such day

As after sunset fadeth in the west,

Which by and by black night doth take away,

Death's second self, that seals up all in rest.

In me thou see'st the glowing of such fire

That on the ashes of his youth doth lie,

As the deathbed whereon it must expire

Consumed with that which it was nourish'd by.

This thou perceiv'st, which makes thy love more strong,

To love that well which thou must leave ere long.

~ WS

73.

The Grim Surveyor lays on me his line,
& all my deeds & titles soon must lie
at rest with me in earth & in your minds,
entombed with that which i had flourished by.

my corpse's cells are rent by what i rent,
re-turned to that which granted me returns.
like rain, i'm re-collected by the trench.
the land re-leases him who once leased her.

i'm re-possessed by what i had possessed,
re-claimed by what my shameless lust had claimed,
interred into what gave me interest,
encompassed now by what my compass tamed.

my tissue-letters writ by chromosomes
now re-arranged to air, sun, sand & foam.

~ JD

LXXIV.

But be contented: when that fell arrest

Without all bail shall carry me away,

My life hath in this line some interest,

Which for memorial still with thee shall stay.

When thou reviewest this, thou dost review

The very part was consecrate to thee:

The earth can have but earth, which is his due;

My spirit is thine, the better part of me:

So then thou hast but lost the dregs of life,

The prey of worms, my body being dead,

The coward conquest of a wretch's knife,

Too base of thee to be remembered.

The worth of that is that which it contains,

And that is this, and this with thee remains.

~ WS

74.

the world is forced to whisper when it snows.

white blankets smother sounds of marketplace.

just so, a stilted silence drifts & floats

above my lifeless corpse & frozen face.

in me you see what someday you will be:

dead. it all seems like a dream to you, this

funeral. rites, interment—decency

demands it. but i am no longer with

you. you whom i loved, how will you incor-

porate my death into your life? what if

your cell phone rings during the service? for-

tunately, you're not the one who's dead. dif-

ferent people deal with these things differently.

is it different this time, now that it's me?

~ JD

LXXV.

So are you to my thoughts as food to life,

Or as sweet-season'd showers are to the ground;

And for the peace of you I hold such strife

As 'twixt a miser and his wealth is found;

Now proud as an enjoyer and anon

Doubting the filching age will steal his treasure,

Now counting best to be with you alone,

Then better'd that the world may see my pleasure;

Sometime all full with feasting on your sight

And by and by clean starved for a look;

Possessing or pursuing no delight,

Save what is had or must from you be took.

Thus do I pine and surfeit day by day,

Or gluttoning on all, or all away.

~ WS

75.

your love is my identity's undoing,

a tapestry of life that you unravel.

you gave me all these projects i'm pursuing—

my stored-up labor, products, & travail.

a torn & time-worn page you write your prose on—

(i'd hibernate in zarathustra's cave

were i not this *zôon politikon)*—

the more i take from you the less i have.

i tighten up my woof in lonely moments,

weaving my self-to-self, self-paid, self-earning.

my frothy drives & knowledge-pools foment

stagnation & a yearning, returning,

for churning social systems that unswirl

my truth, my affirmation of the world.

~ JD

LXXVI.

Why is my verse so barren of new pride,

So far from variation or quick change?

Why with the time do I not glance aside

To new-found methods and to compounds strange?

Why write I still all one, ever the same,

And keep invention in a noted weed,

That every word doth almost tell my name,

Showing their birth and where they did proceed?

O, know, sweet love, I always write of you,

And you and love are still my argument;

So all my best is dressing old words new,

Spending again what is already spent:

For as the sun is daily new and old,

So is my love still telling what is told.

~ WS

76.

these duodactylic & risible lines

perpetuate human identity.

biology-rhythms, content to define

us, transfigure our fragile humanity.

poetry-traces can make human races

revise what they thought was the truth.

as our DNA alters, belief-bases

falter, as language is put to new use...

...by our clowns in high places that scratch at their

faces and try to deny what they are.

still these poets & preachers (philosophy

teachers), demand that we stand at their bar.

but continuity pervades this game—

the more we change, the more we stay the same.

~ JD

LXXVII.

Thy glass will show thee how thy beauties wear,

Thy dial how thy precious minutes waste;

The vacant leaves thy mind's imprint will bear,

And of this book this learning mayst thou taste.

The wrinkles which thy glass will truly show

Of mouthed graves will give thee memory;

Thou by thy dial's shady stealth mayst know

Time's thievish progress to eternity.

Look, what thy memory can not contain

Commit to these waste blanks, and thou shalt find

Those children nursed, deliver'd from thy brain,

To take a new acquaintance of thy mind.

These offices, so oft as thou wilt look,

Shall profit thee and much enrich thy book.

~ WS

77.

the mirror is the place you find your way,

your symmetry, the center of your eye.

your middle course is what you call "today."

"tomorrow" is the day that you will die.

the riddle of the palindrome pervades

your hopes & memories of yesteryear.

the anagrams of all your escapades

in all your social circles breed your fear,

constrain the poetry of every act.

& if the rhythm & the rhyme of your

enchanted soul confound your social pacts,

then be yourself & never ask for more.

the mirror gives your rationality.

your love of life alone will set you free.

~ JD

LXXVIII.

So oft have I invoked thee for my Muse

And found such fair assistance in my verse

As every alien pen hath got my use

And under thee their poesy disperse.

Thine eyes that taught the dumb on high to sing

And heavy ignorance aloft to fly

Have added feathers to the learned's wing

And given grace a double majesty.

Yet be most proud of that which I compile,

Whose influence is thine and born of thee:

In others' works thou dost but mend the style,

And arts with thy sweet graces graced be;

But thou art all my art and dost advance

As high as learning my rude ignorance.

~ WS

78.

fixation is the problem—need & greed—
the teat that you have learned to suckle at.
the anarchy of hunger makes you feed—
the fear of loss, the fear of falling flat.

the diaphragm is built for breath, not fear;
the mind to help you live and help your race.
the secrets of the heart do not appear
within the nauseas of commonplace.

so shed a tear & recollect your soul.
the problem for your steel resolve is rust.
remember once again your highest goal—
the only thing you know that you can trust.

breathe in the only air you'll ever know
to overcome the world you undergo.

~ JD

LXXIX.

Whilst I alone did call upon thy aid,
My verse alone had all thy gentle grace,
But now my gracious numbers are decay'd
And my sick Muse doth give another place.

I grant, sweet love, thy lovely argument
Deserves the travail of a worthier pen,
Yet what of thee thy poet doth invent
He robs thee of and pays it thee again.

He lends thee virtue and he stole that word
From thy behavior; beauty doth he give
And found it in thy cheek; he can afford
No praise to thee but what in thee doth live.

Then thank him not for that which he doth say,
Since what he owes thee thou thyself dost pay.

~ WS

79.

no cup is large enough to hold the sea,

no storehouse vast enough to keep the earth.

so too, your life is boundless, rich, & free

despite these measured words that sound your worth.

translation is a land where much gets lost,

including nuance, rhythm, assonance,

syntax & grammar, phonemes, morphemes—glossed

over like scrawled marginalia. chance-

genes & numerologies lose bases.

how, then, can I decode my love's details?

noticing one trait almost erases

another & my system of symbols

is sure to flatter or to fail your truth.

sememes make sense, but can't refer to you.

~ JD

LXXX.

O, how I faint when I of you do write,

Knowing a better spirit doth use your name,

And in the praise thereof spends all his might,

To make me tongue-tied, speaking of your fame!

But since your worth, wide as the ocean is,

The humble as the proudest sail doth bear,

My saucy bark inferior far to his

On your broad main doth wilfully appear.

Your shallowest help will hold me up afloat,

Whilst he upon your soundless deep doth ride;

Or being wreck'd, I am a worthless boat,

He of tall building and of goodly pride:

Then if he thrive and I be cast away,

The worst was this; my love was my decay.

~ WS

80.

a flood of information comes to us

on airwaves. sign-waves, currents, torrents, bits

of that & undigested bytes of this—

a data-stream against whose banks we're thrust.

what difference then if i decide to float

a fond description over you (unless

perhaps it land me in your port)? fairest

forms of art are now engulfed by speech bloat-

ed with spam. why should i try to drown the

deafening sound & mindless drone with my po-

etic tones? words had matter long ago,

& contact with the depths that they traversed;

but now they hover ghost-like over grounds.

we made words fly by changing them to sounds.

~ JD

LXXXI.

Or I shall live your epitaph to make,

Or you survive when I in earth am rotten;

From hence your memory death cannot take,

Although in me each part will be forgotten.

Your name from hence immortal life shall have,

Though I, once gone, to all the world must die:

The earth can yield me but a common grave,

When you entombed in men's eyes shall lie.

Your monument shall be my gentle verse,

Which eyes not yet created shall o'er-read,

And tongues to be your being shall rehearse

When all the breathers of this world are dead;

You still shall live—such virtue hath my pen—

Where breath most breathes, even in the mouths of men.

~ WS

81.

O Ilium, shake spirits from the graves

Of ancient Greeks! Olympus, reconvene

Your Pantheon! Atlantis, part the waves

And rise again! All hosts of unseen

Hades, breathe & speak! How is this vast &

ghastly mob re-summoned to the graveyard

of our minds? *Their names*, like epitaphs, stand

on the yellowed pages of our grimoires:

our hallowed epics, metaphors, & myths.

The earth does not respect such names as she

recycles corpses. We litter her with

gravestones. So too, our corporate id's mostly

unmarked...save these names: these gazed-on objects,

private properties, phallic obelisks.

~ JD

LXXXII.

I grant thou wert not married to my Muse

And therefore mayst without attaint o'erlook

The dedicated words which writers use

Of their fair subject, blessing every book.

Thou art as fair in knowledge as in hue,

Finding thy worth a limit past my praise,

And therefore art enforced to seek anew

Some fresher stamp of the time-bettering days.

And do so, love; yet when they have devised

What strained touches rhetoric can lend,

Thou truly fair wert truly sympathized

In true plain words by thy true-telling friend;

And their gross painting might be better used

Where cheeks need blood; in thee it is abused.

~ WS

82.

once coined, a word or metaphor or phrase

gains currency & circulates until

its worth's effaced, then commonplace, it fades

into the background noise, inaudible.

man's stamps—his gods & muses, wives & tongues—

once born, these symbols grow, decay & die.

my ancient god, o muse, now fills his lungs

with his last breath, leaves you bereft, his bride,

to bury him. what will you do now that

your lord, your *raison d'être*'s dead? old coin

of dead economy, old widow, what

price does your dead fiat now command? join

me to seek new words, loves, trades, & cultures—

dead love-feasts are for necrophiles & vultures.

~ JD

LXXXIII.

I never saw that you did painting need
And therefore to your fair no painting set;
I found, or thought I found, you did exceed
The barren tender of a poet's debt;

And therefore have I slept in your report,
That you yourself being extant well might show
How far a modern quill doth come too short,
Speaking of worth, what worth in you doth grow.

This silence for my sin you did impute,
Which shall be most my glory, being dumb;
For I impair not beauty being mute,
When others would give life and bring a tomb.

There lives more life in one of your fair eyes
Than both your poets can in praise devise.

~ WS

83.

my letters are but pointless blots & marks,

my sounds but stains upon serenity.

my phrases are deceptions in the dark,

my works an exercise in vanity.

of all the people in this world of mine,

i am the hardest to manipulate.

my life's too rich for poor words to describe,

& language has a beggar's exchange-rate.

i fail to change my will with hollow sounds.

all trade in lexemes is but bet or bribe.

my praise remains an overdrawn account—

die welt als wille und vorstellung bleibt.

but, addict of acclaim, you yearn for more—

crazed with withdrawal from crack-like semaphore.

~ JD

LXXXIV.

Who is it that says most? which can say more
Than this rich praise, that you alone are you?
In whose confine immured is the store
Which should example where your equal grew.

Lean penury within that pen doth dwell
That to his subject lends not some small glory;
But he that writes of you, if he can tell
That you are you, so dignifies his story,

Let him but copy what in you is writ,
Not making worse what nature made so clear,
And such a counterpart shall fame his wit,
Making his style admired every where.

You to your beauteous blessings add a curse,
Being fond on praise, which makes your praises worse.

~ WS

84.

my fashion-forward style of unity is mine alone—

my private shades of meaning that accrue to well-worn words,

or sentimental values i attach to things i own—

outside my skin, my complex impeti appear absurd.

can i describe how solipsistic scripts prescribe my role

& form my character? or is it not enough that i

should act? i show my tensions, role-strains, obstacles & goals

through my behavior on the public stages of my life...

...but consummate my marriage to the world with private tantras.

my penetralia protect momentous holy mantras.

~ JD

LXXXV.

My tongue-tied Muse in manners holds her still,

While comments of your praise, richly compiled,

Reserve their character with golden quill

And precious phrase by all the Muses filed.

I think good thoughts whilst other write good words,

And like unletter'd clerk still cry 'Amen'

To every hymn that able spirit affords

In polish'd form of well-refined pen.

Hearing you praised, I say "'Tis so, 'tis true,"

And to the most of praise add something more;

But that is in my thought, whose love to you,

Though words come hindmost, holds his rank before.

Then others for the breath of words respect,

Me for my dumb thoughts, speaking in effect.

~ WS

85.

god, love, & money are the masks we wear—

the only open roles in this *commed-*

ia dell'arte. the values we share,

each action we perform, each drive & need

& institution comes from some amal-

gamation of these three façades for life.

for virgins, proselytes, & capital?

one house to worship, tithe, or take a wife.

skyscrapers & cathedrals, codices,

stockpiles of wealth & strict moralities—

we spend our blood & sweat & tears on these.

tragedians emote soliloquies.

great apes throw feces. children play their games.

we pray, invest, & wed—it's in our veins.

~ JD

LXXXVI.

Was it the proud full sail of his great verse,

Bound for the prize of all too precious you,

That did my ripe thoughts in my brain inhearse,

Making their tomb the womb wherein they grew?

Was it his spirit, by spirits taught to write

Above a mortal pitch, that struck me dead?

No, neither he, nor his compeers by night

Giving him aid, my verse astonished.

He, nor that affable familiar ghost

Which nightly gulls him with intelligence

As victors of my silence cannot boast;

I was not sick of any fear from thence:

But when your countenance fill'd up his line,

Then lack'd I matter; that enfeebled mine.

~ WS

86.

The center of your soul is my abode.

My cloak the darkness of centrality,

My robe the blood of every muse and hope,

My ghastly gaze denudes duplicity.

My eyes are fire, my face is like the sun.

My laugh is lightning, and my sorcery

Omnipotent and dire. In dreams I come

But once or twice. Remember me. I see

Beneath your deepest dread. (How could I fear?

Instead, beware, O dark! Prepare to meet

Your goal! O bleak abyss, black lonely mist,

The only thing more drear than you is here!)

Suppressed with each banal and busy breath,

Dauntless, I stir: the Truth of your own Death.

~ JD

LXXXVII.

Farewell! thou art too dear for my possessing,

And like enough thou know'st thy estimate:

The charter of thy worth gives thee releasing;

My bonds in thee are all determinate.

For how do I hold thee but by thy granting?

And for that riches where is my deserving?

The cause of this fair gift in me is wanting,

And so my patent back again is swerving.

Thyself thou gavest, thy own worth then not knowing,

Or me, to whom thou gavest it, else mistaking;

So thy great gift, upon misprision growing,

Comes home again, on better judgment making.

Thus have I had thee, as a dream doth flatter,

In sleep a king, but waking no such matter.

~ WS

87.

our cultural unconscious dreams of wealth:

"each piece of gold, a tiny piece of rule."

we corporate zombies toast each other's health:

"si sentio, habeo ergo sum."

la vie: un rêve bref, un mot fini.

si somniat, homo in terra est.

at one with earth most closely in our sleep,

our dream-selves have no reason to possess.

to have, to hold, & having (*being had*)—

in dreams, possession shifts with agency.

perspectives change, & selves are myriad...

...but dawn dispels this common history.

we wake to bank-notes backed by gold & god

& metanarratives of private sod.

LXXXVIII.

When thou shalt be disposed to set me light,

And place my merit in the eye of scorn,

Upon thy side against myself I'll fight,

And prove thee virtuous, though thou art forsworn.

With mine own weakness being best acquainted,

Upon thy part I can set down a story

Of faults conceal'd, wherein I am attainted,

That thou in losing me shalt win much glory:

And I by this will be a gainer too;

For bending all my loving thoughts on thee,

The injuries that to myself I do,

Doing thee vantage, double-vantage me.

Such is my love, to thee I so belong,

That for thy right myself will bear all wrong.

~ WS

88.

since they won't let me live here anymore,

just say the word, & i'll go find new caves—

deep recesses with plenty to explore,

or shallow holes...much easier to leave.

"a bar on every corner," so it seems,

(each group i'm in imposes codes on me).

tribunals of the tribe, the courts of each

clique subpoena me for crimes against the

oldest justice of all: WHAT PEOPLE THINK.

now the blind leaders of your lair declare

that we "profane their images." they blink.

i'll take the blame & banishment from their

cult. here, take my bingo-card for their appro-

val. i won't need it, & plus, you'll have two.

~ JD

V

LXXXIX.

Say that thou didst forsake me for some fault,

And I will comment upon that offence;

Speak of my lameness, and I straight will halt,

Against thy reasons making no defence.

Thou canst not, love, disgrace me half so ill,

To set a form upon desired change,

As I'll myself disgrace: knowing thy will,

I will acquaintance strangle and look strange,

Be absent from thy walks, and in my tongue

Thy sweet beloved name no more shall dwell,

Lest I, too much profane, should do it wrong

And haply of our old acquaintance tell.

For thee against myself I'll vow debate,

For I must ne'er love him whom thou dost hate.

~ WS

89.

consolidate your insecurities.
condense them all into a single sign.
conscribe the sigil that's inuring these
into the entity that you call *mine*.

and if, perchance, you happen to recall
the vast event that made our sorrow real,
sob with the heart that brought us to this fall,
& do not fear the way it makes you feel.

then turn about & look it in the eye
& make your sorrow do a double-take.
your legs themselves have taunted you to fly,
to live your life & love another's sake.

red dice roll out the fate of mice & men.
return to me, my love, my denizen.

~ JD

XC.

Then hate me when thou wilt; if ever, now;

Now, while the world is bent my deeds to cross,

Join with the spite of fortune, make me bow,

And do not drop in for an after-loss:

Ah, do not, when my heart hath 'scaped this sorrow,

Come in the rearward of a conquer'd woe;

Give not a windy night a rainy morrow,

To linger out a purposed overthrow.

If thou wilt leave me, do not leave me last,

When other petty griefs have done their spite

But in the onset come; so shall I taste

At first the very worst of fortune's might,

And other strains of woe, which now seem woe,

Compared with loss of thee will not seem so.

~ WS

90.

eli, eli, lama sabachthani?
lord of my moods, refuge of all my days,
i lie alone, a mangled mass of meat,
since you, my muse, depart your dwellingplace!

an atheist, a beast, a corpse you leave
behind, to face dark night without a soul.
a dreamless sleep draws near to smother me—
composed, compost, a tale already told.

half-beast, half-god in waking & in sleep,
through all my life, my god, you've been with me.
how do you now depart? please stay! i plead!
answer me! ...in this moment, books have ceased.

now friendships, wealth, & houses fade.... *adieu—*
i die, but smile while looking back at you.

~ JD

XCI.

Some glory in their birth, some in their skill,

Some in their wealth, some in their bodies' force,

Some in their garments, though new-fangled ill,

Some in their hawks and hounds, some in their horse;

And every humour hath his adjunct pleasure,

Wherein it finds a joy above the rest:

But these particulars are not my measure;

All these I better in one general best.

Thy love is better than high birth to me,

Richer than wealth, prouder than garments' cost,

Of more delight than hawks or horses be;

And having thee, of all men's pride I boast:

Wretched in this alone, that thou mayst take

All this away and me most wretched make.

~ WS

91.

she drinks her wine. he drinks his gatorade.

she hasn't had her cup of coffee yet.

he just quit smoking & she just got laid.

she's on the rag. he's started working out.

such liturgies pervade their daily lives.

their holiest communions are mundane.

eating & drinking, sex & exercise—

these habit-casuistries *decide* their days.

he hones his body, but she disregards

hers, busy with her soul & church & kids.

he makes his life into a work of art.

she follows jesus. he's an agnostic...

...he lives embodied & refines his tastes.

she pines for her eternal resting-place.

~ JD

XCII.

But do thy worst to steal thyself away,

For term of life thou art assured mine,

And life no longer than thy love will stay,

For it depends upon that love of thine.

Then need I not to fear the worst of wrongs,

When in the least of them my life hath end.

I see a better state to me belongs

Than that which on thy humour doth depend;

Thou canst not vex me with inconstant mind,

Since that my life on thy revolt doth lie.

O, what a happy title do I find,

Happy to have thy love, happy to die!

But what's so blessed-fair that fears no blot?

Thou mayst be false, and yet I know it not.

~ WS

92.

these bursts of passion steal my "self" away.
rhapsodic moments when my memories fade—
insane, ill-humored, human, inhumane—
unweave my ego & the vows it made.

am i a different "i" in ecstasy
(or love or lust or hunger or desire)?
when hormone-chemicals imbalance me,
i feel my subjectivity rewire.

but what does all this have to do with you?
my would-be lover, how you do your hair,
the way you smell, that little thing you do
with your eyebrows, your hypnotizing stare—

these tiny triggers make my passions rise.
my id is kindled, & my ego dies.

~ JD

XCIII.

So shall I live, supposing thou art true,

Like a deceived husband; so love's face

May still seem love to me, though alter'd new;

Thy looks with me, thy heart in other place:

For there can live no hatred in thine eye,

Therefore in that I cannot know thy change.

In many's looks the false heart's history

Is writ in moods and frowns and wrinkles strange,

But heaven in thy creation did decree

That in thy face sweet love should ever dwell;

Whate'er thy thoughts or thy heart's workings be,

Thy looks should nothing thence but sweetness tell.

How like Eve's apple doth thy beauty grow,

if thy sweet virtue answer not thy show!

~ WS

93.

before earth was dissected by our places,

adam & eve forged our hearts. their gold-smith's

seal still informs our mettle & worn faces.

their demi-urges shaped our prime objectives.

the numbers dance & in their cosmic laws

we find our private numerologies,

our names & tickers in the cryptic wash

of chaotic symbols...& we're happy.

the masses dance. we add our mass to theirs,

& weigh ourselves against them silently.

the bodies dance. we gyrate, each a ware

of world cash-flow, priced individually.

the meanings dance. we pick some, investing

our inward hoards with selective meanings.

XCIV.

They that have power to hurt and will do none,
That do not do the thing they most do show,
Who, moving others, are themselves as stone,
Unmoved, cold, and to temptation slow,

They rightly do inherit heaven's graces
And husband nature's riches from expense;
They are the lords and owners of their faces,
Others but stewards of their excellence.

The summer's flower is to the summer sweet,
Though to itself it only live and die,
But if that flower with base infection meet,
The basest weed outbraves his dignity:

For sweetest things turn sourest by their deeds;
Lilies that fester smell far worse than weeds.

~ WS

94.

with power comes responsibility.
the teeth of tigers & the claws of men,
by drive, desire, passion, urge, or need,
crave blood. no king-of-beasts asserts ascend-
ancy without the slaughter of its prey.

where maggot-swarms undo dead-lion-manes,
unsung, pervasive power-networks play.

ant-rhythms tell the time of the insane.
new lines of force, ubiquitous, unseen,
like suns & moons, have measured out our times—
symbolic / real / imaginary means—
the art of the ridiculous sublime.

where power, money, time, & life combine,
what agency-remains can i call "mine"?

~ JD

XCV.

How sweet and lovely dost thou make the shame

Which, like a canker in the fragrant rose,

Doth spot the beauty of thy budding name!

O, in what sweets dost thou thy sins enclose!

That tongue that tells the story of thy days,

Making lascivious comments on thy sport,

Cannot dispraise but in a kind of praise;

Naming thy name blesses an ill report.

O, what a mansion have those vices got

Which for their habitation chose out thee,

Where beauty's veil doth cover every blot,

And all things turn to fair that eyes can see!

Take heed, dear heart, of this large privilege;

The hardest knife ill-used doth lose his edge.

~ WS

95.

the "lie" that hides my muscles is my skin.
my tissue-difference-inconsistencies
offend your law that "out" should mirror "in,"
your code of strict homogeneity.

should influenza victims be deformed?
or festive garb denied to somber souls?
...not if my moods depend on what i've worn!
despite backstage, a show is just a show.

i acted. what i did is what i did.
my viewers never saw what was "inside."
i am the deed, not the "ego" or "id."
in deed, some things i show & some i hide.

you'd say i've sinned. i'd say "i have survived."
my contradictions prove that i'm alive.

~ JD

XCVI.

Some say thy fault is youth, some wantonness;

Some say thy grace is youth and gentle sport;

Both grace and faults are loved of more and less;

Thou mak'st faults graces that to thee resort.

As on the finger of a throned queen

The basest jewel will be well esteem'd,

So are those errors that in thee are seen

To truths translated and for true things deem'd.

How many lambs might the stern wolf betray,

If like a lamb he could his looks translate!

How many gazers mightst thou lead away,

If thou wouldst use the strength of all thy state!

But do not so; I love thee in such sort

As, thou being mine, mine is thy good report.

~ WS

96.

translation is a land where much gets lost.

when, poet, you're translated into me,

some say our soul's communion is a "gloss."

some say "dissemination is obscene."

our love is transference. like metaphors,

our spirits blend above a sea of "is."

& every friend & lover feels this force—

"his being becomes hers; her being, his."

"these halting feet have run for all & none

of you...of me." our unseen foes proscribe

our love with the waves of their oblivion....

& you, late friend, still will to haunt my lines—

but do not so; i love thee in such sort

as, thou being mine, mine is thy good report.

~ JD

XCVII.

How like a winter hath my absence been

From thee, the pleasure of the fleeting year!

What freezings have I felt, what dark days seen!

What old December's bareness every where!

And yet this time removed was summer's time,

The teeming autumn, big with rich increase,

Bearing the wanton burden of the prime,

Like widow'd wombs after their lords' decease:

Yet this abundant issue seem'd to me

But hope of orphans and unfather'd fruit;

For summer and his pleasures wait on thee,

And, thou away, the very birds are mute;

Or, if they sing, 'tis with so dull a cheer

That leaves look pale, dreading the winter's near.

~ WS

97.

i chase my single arc from dark to dark

where worlds create themselves & are unmade

ex nihilo from your distance, vital star,

until the day my final shadows fade.

we thought it grand, when, hand in hand, we scorched

the steamy equinox. ...until at last,

bright sun-green grass fell to the herbivore,

tundra for the dream-molars of the past.

with you afar, i face my final freeze.

my coldest solstices coagulate.

conjured conjectures, traced trajectories,

once made me smile as we traversed our way.

but now, de-centered by my star's retreat,

i sip my sun's last rays with heavy feet.

~ JD

XCVIII.

From you have I been absent in the spring,

When proud-pied April dress'd in all his trim

Hath put a spirit of youth in every thing,

That heavy Saturn laugh'd and leap'd with him.

Yet nor the lays of birds nor the sweet smell

Of different flowers in odour and in hue

Could make me any summer's story tell,

Or from their proud lap pluck them where they grew;

Nor did I wonder at the lily's white,

Nor praise the deep vermilion in the rose;

They were but sweet, but figures of delight,

Drawn after you, you pattern of all those.

Yet seem'd it winter still, and, you away,

As with your shadow I with these did play:

~ WS

98.

you fuck me. we don't make love anymore.

because fuck doesn't have a face. all the

objects of your anger & your lust are

just as generic as they are arbitrary.

you never look at me. you look away,

because what you love is the archetype—

male, tall, tight body, a mind... you fixate.

these qualities make you horny. but why?

am i your pornographic fantasy—

faceless, defaced, replaced with images?

you also like romantic comedies.

your ideal man is formed by these fictitious

tales. he gives roses & cries in movies.

you make love to this ken-doll. you fuck me.

~ JD

XCIX.

The forward violet thus did I chide:

Sweet thief, whence didst thou steal thy sweet that smells,
If not from my love's breath? The purple pride
Which on thy soft cheek for complexion dwells
In my love's veins thou hast too grossly dyed.

The lily I condemned for thy hand,
And buds of marjoram had stol'n thy hair:
The roses fearfully on thorns did stand,
One blushing shame, another white despair;

A third, nor red nor white, had stol'n of both
And to his robbery had annex'd thy breath;
But, for his theft, in pride of all his growth
A vengeful canker eat him up to death.

More flowers I noted, yet I none could see
But sweet or colour it had stol'n from thee.

~ WS

99.

"colorless green ideas sleep furiously!"

unripe, delightful innocence of love!

from feeling blastocoels: "a head!" ...then "feet!"

chromatophores: "below? so too above!"

i love what infants do inside your pants.

in you the child is mother of the dream.

you hunt like crocodiles and flirt like ants.

your bright eyes leap with your night-lemur teams.

a fury flows through those night-knowing limbs

whose taut discomforts give position-change,

whose sinews, strung by sunny-organisms,

reprise motifs for moontime's hearing range.

i love you just because you are this child:

who brings to garden only from the wild.

~ JD

C.

Where art thou, Muse, that thou forget'st so long

To speak of that which gives thee all thy might?

Spend'st thou thy fury on some worthless song,

Darkening thy power to lend base subjects light?

Return, forgetful Muse, and straight redeem

In gentle numbers time so idly spent;

Sing to the ear that doth thy lays esteem

And gives thy pen both skill and argument.

Rise, resty Muse, my love's sweet face survey,

If Time have any wrinkle graven there;

If any, be a satire to decay,

And make Time's spoils despised everywhere.

Give my love fame faster than Time wastes life;

So thou prevent'st his scythe and crooked knife.

~ WS

100.

the tentacles of will entangle us:

we only hear what we are meant to hear.

to taste the fruits of dreams & consciousness:

the inner eye becomes the inner ear.

remember when you miscommunicate:

the horsemen standing ready at the door.

the fear is never larger than the fate:

"tomorrow" is another word for "more."

retrace your steps to find me once again:

a circle always feels its center-point.

the daughters are the brides, the boys are men:

desire drips its oil to anoint.

now is your time to turn into the light:

forever is your blindness & your sight.

~ JD

CI.

O truant Muse, what shall be thy amends
For thy neglect of truth in beauty dyed?
Both truth and beauty on my love depends;
So dost thou too, and therein dignified.

Make answer, Muse: wilt thou not haply say
'Truth needs no colour, with his colour fix'd;
Beauty no pencil, beauty's truth to lay;
But best is best, if never intermix'd?'

Because he needs no praise, wilt thou be dumb?
Excuse not silence so; for't lies in thee
To make him much outlive a gilded tomb,
And to be praised of ages yet to be.

Then do thy office, Muse; I teach thee how
To make him seem long hence as he shows now.

~ WS

101.

can words describe the color of your soul?

...still, each beholder's eyes behold your truth,

engraved by beauty's timeless ratios.

your life is true. why should i write of you?

...unless to multiply embodiments,

investing you into my metaphors—

new second-selves, new lyrical events—

substantiating you into my words.

an actor, you're the sum of all your parts.

your character is formed by roles you've played,

possessing bodies by this magic art—

the essence of the maker in the made.

your corpse will turn to melons, maize, & mice.

the letter kills. the metaphor gives life.

~ JD

CII.

My love is strengthen'd, though more weak in seeming;

I love not less, though less the show appear:

That love is merchandized whose rich esteeming

The owner's tongue doth publish every where.

Our love was new, and then but in the spring,

When I was wont to greet it with my lays,

As Philomel in summer's front doth sing

And stops her pipe in growth of riper days:

Not that the summer is less pleasant now

Than when her mournful hymns did hush the night,

But that wild music burthens every bough

And sweets grown common lose their dear delight.

Therefore like her I sometime hold my tongue,

Because I would not dull you with my song.

~ WS

102.

who is this author-ideality

that speaks to you beyond & on the page,

whose words are backed by your authority,

a pupil to the eyes these words engage?

the poet is incarnate in the poem.

the reader too. take. read. this is my flesh

& blood i give for you. ingest this tome,

the author-worldly banquet of this text.

but you, my love—my reader & my theme—

you have a double-body in my verse.

exposed to my poetic hopes & dreams,

the unpaid actor-voyeur of my words.

my dreams unearth your silent nudities,

my rhymes, your real-life metamorphoses.

~ JD

CIII.

Alack, what poverty my Muse brings forth,

That having such a scope to show her pride,

The argument all bare is of more worth

Than when it hath my added praise beside!

O, blame me not, if I no more can write!

Look in your glass, and there appears a face

That over-goes my blunt invention quite,

Dulling my lines and doing me disgrace.

Were it not sinful then, striving to mend,

To mar the subject that before was well?

For to no other pass my verses tend

Than of your graces and your gifts to tell;

And more, much more, than in my verse can sit

Your own glass shows you when you look in it.

~ WS

103.

you've heard, "in the beginning was the Word."

the Word was with the Muse, and was the Muse.

the Word became the Meaning of the earth,

the light that every human life must use.

the Muse, the Meaning, and the Word are one.

since Meaning comes from bard and reader, then,

"the poet is the poem" is the pun—

and you and I make Word and Muse make sense.

but now my Muse and Word are Meaningless

against your naked body's argument.

my syllogisms stretch to timelessness

the beauty that your body has condensed.

your naked premises beat my conclusions—

like narcissus forgets—art is illusion.

~ JD

CIV.

To me, fair friend, you never can be old,

For as you were when first your eye I eyed,

Such seems your beauty still. Three winters cold

Have from the forests shook three summers' pride,

Three beauteous springs to yellow autumn turn'd

In process of the seasons have I seen,

Three April perfumes in three hot Junes burn'd,

Since first I saw you fresh, which yet are green.

Ah! yet doth beauty, like a dial-hand,

Steal from his figure and no pace perceived;

So your sweet hue, which methinks still doth stand,

Hath motion and mine eye may be deceived:

For fear of which, hear this, thou age unbred;

Ere you were born was beauty's summer dead.

~ WS

104.

ask not for whom the bell tolls. ask, "for what?"
it tolls for time. time past. completed time.
it doesn't toll time's wheel. it tolls a rut—
what seemed a ray, the segment of a line.

it doesn't toll a go. it tolls a went.
a corpse, cadaver; broken factory
for making cash; closed atm; a spent
amount of hours, powers, capital, & needs.

the deeds are done. the deal is shaken on,
condensed & frozen in a final breath.
recipients rejoice: their patron's gone;
& beneficiaries dance your death.

the earth devours your cells...your heirs, your stores—
assessing all the things that once were yours.

~ JD

CV.

Let not my love be call'd idolatry,

Nor my beloved as an idol show,

Since all alike my songs and praises be

To one, of one, still such, and ever so.

Kind is my love to-day, to-morrow kind,

Still constant in a wondrous excellence;

Therefore my verse to constancy confined,

One thing expressing, leaves out difference.

'Fair, kind and true' is all my argument,

'Fair, kind, and true' varying to other words;

And in this change is my invention spent,

Three themes in one, which wondrous scope affords.

'Fair, kind, and true,' have often lived alone,

Which three till now never kept seat in one.

~ WS

105.

I love you, neighbor, like I love myself.

One love, one care, directed at my core.

Since "no one ever hated his own flesh,"

I love my skin; my kin by metaphor.

To my own self I must be kind & true.

The god behind my veil of consciousness

Demands the homage of an introvert,

And fairness to myself is a reflex.

My love, you live beside my Being's house,

Where all my yesterdays become today,

This tenement by which time's waters pass,

This tent whose ground creates my time & space.

Come share my fire, my friend. Come share my love—

Unmoved & one—around which all things move.

~ JD

CVI.

When in the chronicle of wasted time

I see descriptions of the fairest wights,

And beauty making beautiful old rhyme

In praise of ladies dead and lovely knights,

Then, in the blazon of sweet beauty's best,

Of hand, of foot, of lip, of eye, of brow,

I see their antique pen would have express'd

Even such a beauty as you master now.

So all their praises are but prophecies

Of this our time, all you prefiguring;

And, for they look'd but with divining eyes,

They had not skill enough your worth to sing:

For we, which now behold these present days,

Have eyes to wonder, but lack tongues to praise.

~ WS

106.

my beauty lives. why do you then lament

that I must walk among the wastes of time—

dungheaps where you, my bard-historian,

eliminate my life into your rhymes?

recycled matter takes poetic form.

meanwhile, my body burns time's calories.

the peristalsis of the universe

churns out the time that nourishes my needs.

the times you waste become a fecal mass,

organic temporal traces, residues.

your dearest hopes & fears? these too shall pass.

my body & its time become your food.

what nutrients you'll take from me—who knows?

my questions open what your answers close.

~ JD

CVII.

Not mine own fears, nor the prophetic soul

Of the wide world dreaming on things to come,

Can yet the lease of my true love control,

Supposed as forfeit to a confined doom.

The mortal moon hath her eclipse endured

And the sad augurs mock their own presage;

Incertainties now crown themselves assured

And peace proclaims olives of endless age.

Now with the drops of this most balmy time

My love looks fresh, and death to me subscribes,

Since, spite of him, I'll live in this poor rhyme,

While he insults o'er dull and speechless tribes:

And thou in this shalt find thy monument,

When tyrants' crests and tombs of brass are spent.

~ WS

107.

cold white envelops lines of stony black.

acute grave-marks accentuate the plain,

black-rune memorials littering these tracts—

crisp, snow-white sheets spread over beds of slain.

black corpses lie beneath dead-letter slates

where vibrant lives & grass & sunshine shone.

now meaning for these lives evaporates—

reduced & metamorphed into a stone.

deathbeds of meaning marked by frigid cairns—

what plots climax at this necropolis?

my thought by hard return might enter here

if shades of meaning haunt such monoliths.

it's winter. i imagine dying leaves

one lying frozen in a senseless grave.

~ JD

CVIII.

What's in the brain that ink may character

Which hath not figured to thee my true spirit?

What's new to speak, what new to register,

That may express my love or thy dear merit?

Nothing, sweet boy; but yet, like prayers divine,

I must each day say o'er the very same,

Counting no old thing old, thou mine, I thine,

Even as when first I hallow'd thy fair name.

So that eternal love in love's fresh case

Weighs not the dust and injury of age,

Nor gives to necessary wrinkles place,

But makes antiquity for aye his page,

Finding the first conceit of love there bred

Where time and outward form would show it dead.

~ WS

108.

when "pro," i'm -*scribed* by all my -*creations*.

when "circum," -*vented* by my -*locutors*.

when "contra," i am -*vened* by my -*dictions*.

when "meta," all my -*physics* become -*phors*.

when "con," my -*cepts* & -*clusions* all seem -*trived*.

when "be," my -*havior* always -*lies* my -*liefs*.

when "a," -*gnostics* are -*mused* that i'm still -*live*.

when "sub," my -*jective* world's a -*poena* (-*tly*)

when "in," my -*terpretations* all seem -*ane*—

since social -*structions* of -*sidious* -*tent*

-*ure*, -*vade*, & -*veigle* my -*genuous* brain,

my -*stincts*, -*tuitions*, -*klings*, & -*telligence*.

when "i," my -*dols* & -*cons* laugh -*ronically*

as -, -*gnorant*, become my -*ambs* & -*deals*.

~ JD

CIX.

O, never say that I was false of heart,

Though absence seem'd my flame to qualify.

As easy might I from myself depart

As from my soul, which in thy breast doth lie:

That is my home of love: if I have ranged,

Like him that travels I return again,

Just to the time, not with the time exchanged,

So that myself bring water for my stain.

Never believe, though in my nature reign'd

All frailties that besiege all kinds of blood,

That it could so preposterously be stain'd,

To leave for nothing all thy sum of good;

For nothing this wide universe I call,

Save thou, my rose; in it thou art my all.

~ WS

109.

darkness oozes all about, around, be-
neath my footpads falling on the forest
floor. i roam, a banished creature of the
night, seeking my home and my certain dest-

iny. my soft black absorbs the silent
of the path till finally the pitch of
tree-dark opens to the silver-violet
moonlight. my home at last! the grasslands! cov-

ered by the grass there, too, my very own
gazelle! who would disturb her majestic
beauty from its wonderful, naïve, lone-
ly sleep? my heart throbs blood now hot and stick-

y to my pounding head—her form the cause—
i shiver...and *pounce* with extended claws.

~ JD

CX.

Alas, 'tis true I have gone here and there

And made myself a motley to the view,

Gored mine own thoughts, sold cheap what is most dear,

Made old offences of affections new;

Most true it is that I have look'd on truth

Askance and strangely: but, by all above,

These blenches gave my heart another youth,

And worse essays proved thee my best of love.

Now all is done, have what shall have no end:

Mine appetite I never more will grind

On newer proof, to try an older friend,

A god in love, to whom I am confined.

Then give me welcome, next my heaven the best,

Even to thy pure and most most loving breast.

~ WS

110.

my wisdom's come from doing foolish things—
i've re-economized my very soul,
served under serfs, manipulated kings.
i've eaten worldviews from a ramen-bowl.

i've looked & seen my own eyes looking back—
(from soups, to kings, to serfs, to yester-me)
transcribed my love to a thousand zodiacs
beyond the wastelands of morality.

i test my promises against my time...
where all my knowledge turns hypothesis,
where mouths i've kissed malign as soon as i'm
reborn: a heraclitean phoenix.

so now i fly from rocks of "know" and "true"
...not knowing how the air i breathe is you.

~ JD

VI

CXI.

O, for my sake do you with Fortune chide,

The guilty goddess of my harmful deeds,

That did not better for my life provide

Than public means which public manners breeds.

Thence comes it that my name receives a brand,

And almost thence my nature is subdued

To what it works in, like the dyer's hand:

Pity me then and wish I were renew'd;

Whilst, like a willing patient, I will drink

Potions of eisell 'gainst my strong infection

No bitterness that I will bitter think,

Nor double penance, to correct correction.

Pity me then, dear friend, and I assure ye

Even that your pity is enough to cure me.

~ WS

111.

if i could pluck the stars from out your eyes,

(you'd see that my elixirs are like yours),

or parse the hesitance in your replies

into 1,000 sparkling gymnospores;

if i could bid the sun remind the moon

that stars & planets conjugate the same,

or ask the evening to recall the noon

where revolutions find *themselves* to blame;

then you & i would find an even course,

unburdened by our insecurities,

& jedi would be jedi, force be force;

& hand in hand, we'd seek our purities.

so look into my eyes & know: you're free.

released in heart & mind from tyranny.

~ JD

CXII.

Your love and pity doth the impression fill

Which vulgar scandal stamp'd upon my brow;

For what care I who calls me well or ill,

So you o'er-green my bad, my good allow?

You are my all the world, and I must strive

To know my shames and praises from your tongue:

None else to me, nor I to none alive,

That my steel'd sense or changes right or wrong.

In so profound abysm I throw all care

Of others' voices, that my adder's sense

To critic and to flatterer stopped are.

Mark how with my neglect I do dispense:

You are so strongly in my purpose bred

That all the world besides methinks are dead.

~ WS

112.

they stamped my forehead with the mark of cain

before my birth, before i had a chance—

my gender, race, & economic plane;

my place in all the world, my *différance*.

and when, my love, you were my mountain peak,

i felt like i was king of all the world.

and in my mind our love was my retreat,

beyond the goods & evils of the herd.

but, love, inside your pity's deep abyss,

i saw my pitiful excuse for love.

your sympathy showed me my cowardice:

that all the world—that "they"—must be enough.

so now, our strength will not be satisfied

until our all the world be edified.

~ JD

CXIII.

Since I left you, mine eye is in my mind;

And that which governs me to go about

Doth part his function and is partly blind,

Seems seeing, but effectually is out;

For it no form delivers to the heart

Of bird, of flower, or shape, which it doth latch:

Of his quick objects hath the mind no part,

Nor his own vision holds what it doth catch:

For if it see the rudest or gentlest sight,

The most sweet favour or deformed'st creature,

The mountain or the sea, the day or night,

The crow or dove, it shapes them to your feature:

Incapable of more, replete with you,

My most true mind thus makes mine eye untrue.

~ WS

113.

till i met you, my "i" was in my "mine."

my mind made existential currency

from constant flows of thoughts & stimuli,

amassing its coined capital in "me."

but then i met your fierce, flirtatious glance.

you penetrated me without consent,

possessed my being with your pupils' dance,

& raped my mind of all its arguments.

so now you're all i ever think about.

you're there in every taste and touch and smell.

you're all i see and hear, inside and out.

you've made my life this heaven and this hell.

i'm yours, my love, and i'll spare no expense,

till love blend us in being, mind, and sense.

~ JD

CXIV.

Or whether doth my mind, being crown'd with you,

Drink up the monarch's plague, this flattery?

Or whether shall I say, mine eye saith true,

And that your love taught it this alchemy,

To make of monsters and things indigest

Such cherubins as your sweet self resemble,

Creating every bad a perfect best,

As fast as objects to his beams assemble?

O,'tis the first; 'tis flattery in my seeing,

And my great mind most kingly drinks it up:

Mine eye well knows what with his gust is 'greeing,

And to his palate doth prepare the cup:

If it be poison'd, 'tis the lesser sin

That mine eye loves it and doth first begin.

~ WS

114.

when you're some random bits of stimuli,

my mental categories filter you.

or when you walk into my lifeworld, i

remember & imagine what we do.

but when i love you, hermes goes to sleep.

"interpretation" cannot be the word

for how my senses shift instinctively—

your beauty's focused, blemishes are blurred.

the visible & the invisible

exists as rods & cones & neurons have it.

you see my lips. you see them kissable.

so live by instinct! but first, get good habits.

to see in love is seeing as love sees—

love makes its own epistemologies.

~ JD

CXV.

Those lines that I before have writ do lie,

Even those that said I could not love you dearer:

Yet then my judgment knew no reason why

My most full flame should afterwards burn clearer.

But reckoning time, whose million'd accidents

Creep in 'twixt vows and change decrees of kings,

Tan sacred beauty, blunt the sharp'st intents,

Divert strong minds to the course of altering things;

Alas, why, fearing of time's tyranny,

Might I not then say 'Now I love you best,'

When I was certain o'er incertainty,

Crowning the present, doubting of the rest?

Love is a babe; then might I not say so,

To give full growth to that which still doth grow?

~ WS

115.

i took the crown from the tyrant's head. i spread—

spitting corpses like lead, invested with shreds

of me. i die a million times a day—

reify my fire into iron clichés.

i'm a lava flow dropping igneous rocks,

hard-and-soft, on-and-off. I AM TIME. i clock

internal temperatures & rhyme with limestone-

specks. rhythm's my effect, not cause. i own

my fate & won't apologize for changes

i make, or laws i break, or lives i take

with me to the grave. i make gravity

behave. my flames create with love & strife:

I AM LIFE, turning words & relations to ash—

my tongue is for the future, not the past.

~ JD

CXVI.

Let me not to the marriage of true minds

Admit impediments. Love is not love

Which alters when it alteration finds,

Or bends with the remover to remove:

O no! it is an ever-fixed mark

That looks on tempests and is never shaken;

It is the star to every wandering bark,

Whose worth's unknown, although his height be taken.

Love's not Time's fool, though rosy lips and cheeks

Within his bending sickle's compass come:

Love alters not with his brief hours and weeks,

But bears it out even to the edge of doom.

If this be error and upon me proved,

I never writ, nor no man ever loved.

~ WS

116.

our bodies find new kinds of intercourse.

we—mommy, daddy, mentor, friend—commune

(although mutation mar your lines of force

or find my protean nucleus unhewn

some morning with the torment of human-

ity). the cords that bind two hearts via

shared values or ideals can't bear the strain

of strife...though once this was *our* formula,

too, our world chained to an ideal. far subt-

ler now is our erotic love. stars burn

for stars. my flames lick your heart, lust for what

you will become. so, fueled with values, yearn,

bright star of love, you'll touch my inmost place,

though we be split by interstellar space.

~ JD

CXVII.

Accuse me thus: that I have scanted all

Wherein I should your great deserts repay,

Forgot upon your dearest love to call,

Whereto all bonds do tie me day by day;

That I have frequent been with unknown minds

And given to time your own dear-purchased right

That I have hoisted sail to all the winds

Which should transport me farthest from your sight.

Book both my wilfulness and errors down

And on just proof surmise accumulate;

Bring me within the level of your frown,

But shoot not at me in your waken'd hate;

Since my appeal says I did strive to prove

The constancy and virtue of your love.

117.

so kick my ass and take my name. okay.

don't think my ass is sorry for this shit.

i flipped the script, but baby, it's your play.

forget the audience, babe. this is it.

i burned you like a cigarette. the pain

i gave i don't regret. you made me hard,

i made you wet. but baby, that's the way

it goes. tyler durden sends his regards.

get jealous. ask me all your questions. then,

when you have let my answers calm your fears,

when you can listen with your mouth, my pen

will put one question to your eyes: whose ears?

whose are my ears? then let them be. and let

the freedom that you give be what you get.

~ JD

CXVIII.

Like as, to make our appetites more keen,

With eager compounds we our palate urge,

As, to prevent our maladies unseen,

We sicken to shun sickness when we purge,

Even so, being full of your ne'er-cloying sweetness,

To bitter sauces did I frame my feeding

And, sick of welfare, found a kind of meetness

To be diseased ere that there was true needing.

Thus policy in love, to anticipate

The ills that were not, grew to faults assured

And brought to medicine a healthful state

Which, rank of goodness, would by ill be cured:

But thence I learn, and find the lesson true,

Drugs poison him that so fell sick of you.

~ WS

118.

your life-events flow into you like drugs.

your body tells you everything it needs.

you need your marijuana. i need hugs.

(but every stimulus is wheat-and-weeds....)

extract the evil eye! the evil juice!

and in becoming your experience,

forgive my love for playing fast and loose;

and let your judgment check your recompense!

push paranoia into overdrive!

feed chronos all the stones that you can get:

pain, self-absorption, fear, and other lies!

your "now" is sick of all you can't forget.

your body has a healthy appetite.

let it decide what tastes are wrong and right.

CXIX.

What potions have I drunk of Siren tears,

Distill'd from limbecks foul as hell within,

Applying fears to hopes and hopes to fears,

Still losing when I saw myself to win!

What wretched errors hath my heart committed,

Whilst it hath thought itself so blessed never!

How have mine eyes out of their spheres been fitted

In the distraction of this madding fever!

O benefit of ill! now I find true

That better is by evil still made better;

And ruin'd love, when it is built anew,

Grows fairer than at first, more strong, far greater.

So I return rebuked to my content

And gain by ill thrice more than I have spent.

~ WS

119.

i love myself—i love this store of days

dissected into secondhand tick-tocks.

i think in time-card-ink till my next raise.

my dreams are drunk on the punch of time-clocks.

my formula's a function of my wealth.

my talent's told on tabs & tally-sheets.

my cell's mitosis? microsoft excel.

my time is money—dollars for heartbeats.

the how of time is in its measurement—

mensura homo, product of my times;

my mind pulses my work-environment's

pace—its rates & rhythms. ...but more so, i'm

self-made—pervaded by proclivities

to self-increase my product(ivity).

CXX.

That you were once unkind befriends me now,

And for that sorrow which I then did feel

Needs must I under my transgression bow,

Unless my nerves were brass or hammer'd steel.

For if you were by my unkindness shaken

As I by yours, you've pass'd a hell of time,

And I, a tyrant, have no leisure taken

To weigh how once I suffered in your crime.

O, that our night of woe might have remember'd

My deepest sense, how hard true sorrow hits,

And soon to you, as you to me, then tender'd

The humble slave which wounded bosoms fits!

But that your trespass now becomes a fee;

Mine ransoms yours, and yours must ransom me.

~ WS

120.

i made myself a promise to be true.

i made myself a truth. you made you mine.

i promised you myself. you promised you.

but truth & selves & promises take time.

but time takes truth & selves & promises—

and caught up in the moment, i gave in.

my love was conquered by stolen kisses

and by desire (where truth is imitation).

we compare ourselves to other people.

we act; and for our human audience,

our acts create the world of how they'll treat us,

whose laws & forces come from our performance.

and in your cosmic relativity,

my foul's as fair as when you first fouled me.

~ JD

CXXI.

'Tis better to be vile than vile esteem'd,

When not to be receives reproach of being,

And the just pleasure lost which is so deem'd

Not by our feeling but by others' seeing:

For why should others' false adulterate eyes

Give salutation to my sportive blood?

Or on my frailties why are frailer spies,

Which in their wills count bad what I think good?

No, I am that I am, and they that level

At my abuses reckon up their own:

I may be straight, though they themselves be bevel;

By their rank thoughts my deeds must not be shown;

Unless this general evil they maintain,

All men are bad, and in their badness reign.

~ WS

121.

have i just sinned? have i been indiscreet?

have i transgressed your solemn etiquettes?

what rules in whose game make you say i "cheat"?

whose holy code should teach me to regret?

i fuck & frolic & enjoy my time.

my friends of virtue dance. my wisdom sings.

your spotless bodies hide malignant minds,

whose voyeur-powers come from gyges' ring.

you call my naked truth "pornography."

my lack of artifice incites your rage.

your cancer answers my oncology.

my smiling tigers mock your paper cage.

to those with ears: i seek fellow creators

who are neither rapists nor masturbators.

~ JD

CXXII.

Thy gift, thy tables, are within my brain

Full character'd with lasting memory,

Which shall above that idle rank remain

Beyond all date, even to eternity;

Or at the least, so long as brain and heart

Have faculty by nature to subsist;

Till each to razed oblivion yield his part

Of thee, thy record never can be miss'd.

That poor retention could not so much hold,

Nor need I tallies thy dear love to score;

Therefore to give them from me was I bold,

To trust those tables that receive thee more:

To keep an adjunct to remember thee

Were to import forgetfulness in me.

~ WS

122.

your mind, o humankind, does not compute.

your code refers to programs never built.

<GOTO "absolute truth">? an empty root.

<IF "empty," RUN "dogma.dll">

you download system files to optimize,

though each of you's a singular command,

a unique operation on past lines,

(your product id is your SSN.)

what you call "paranormal episodes"

are frames that play beyond your refresh-rates.

you integrate, archive, & hide your codes.

you run & forget your answer-updates.

so searching is your sole activity—

<FOR LOOP "humanity.exe">

~ JD

CXXIII.

No, Time, thou shalt not boast that I do change:

Thy pyramids built up with newer might

To me are nothing novel, nothing strange;

They are but dressings of a former sight.

Our dates are brief, and therefore we admire

What thou dost foist upon us that is old,

And rather make them born to our desire

Than think that we before have heard them told.

Thy registers and thee I both defy,

Not wondering at the present nor the past,

For thy records and what we see doth lie,

Made more or less by thy continual haste.

This I do vow and this shall ever be;

I will be true, despite thy scythe and thee.

~ WS

123.

time's sickle pops off fickle fatherhoods,

medusas of the mind called *memories:*

(my hydra-headed private histories?)

the palingeneses of all my shoulds.

$a^2 + b^2 = c^2$? ruse!

my "past" opposes & my "now" adjects.

untied from sides, i fly: hypotenuse!

i am the future! project, intersect!

i wait. i'm here to listen and to learn.

i sit in silence, waiting to create.

both then and now flow in. the candle burns.

my paradox: i'm freedom & i'm fate.

so, time, come walk with me, and we shall change—

till we, as lovers, share: a single name.

~ JD

CXXIV.

If my dear love were but the child of state,

It might for Fortune's bastard be unfather'd

As subject to Time's love or to Time's hate,

Weeds among weeds, or flowers with flowers gather'd.

No, it was builded far from accident;

It suffers not in smiling pomp, nor falls

Under the blow of thralled discontent,

Whereto the inviting time our fashion calls:

It fears not policy, that heretic,

Which works on leases of short-number'd hours,

But all alone stands hugely politic,

That it nor grows with heat nor drowns with showers.

To this I witness call the fools of time,

Which die for goodness, who have lived for crime.

~ WS

124.

because of this, my love for you will last.

my love is will, and will is freedom's cot.

you are my will, not now or in the past,

but till my cells feed weeds in flower-pots.

you're never just a means that suits my end.

if you were just a country or a law,

i could dispense with you, or i could spend

your minutes like a trader sells a stock.

one end befalls the one who's meant to die.

but i am meant to *live* until that date.

each moment is a moment I decide:

i want you in my freedom and my fate.

my vow is witnessed by these "fools of time"—

my *moments* speak my love more than my rhyme.

~ JD

CXXV.

Were 't aught to me I bore the canopy,

With my extern the outward honouring,

Or laid great bases for eternity,

Which prove more short than waste or ruining?

Have I not seen dwellers on form and favour

Lose all, and more, by paying too much rent,

For compound sweet forgoing simple savour,

Pitiful thrivers, in their gazing spent?

No, let me be obsequious in thy heart,

And take thou my oblation, poor but free,

Which is not mix'd with seconds, knows no art,

But mutual render, only me for thee.

Hence, thou suborn'd informer! a true soul

When most impeach'd stands least in thy control.

~ WS

125.

new tasks confront my existential stores,

& in these trials of my character,

my gut-reactions show what i've become.

the ultimata of today have met my value-set.

my freedom called them "choices," but my fate

called them "configurations" of the world

& my persona. *sum ergo volo.*

free choices: spontaneous reactions

between two reagents—my character

& today's challenges—though both of these

were mixed & concentrated yesterday.

i'm one suspension, one solution for

my problems & my choices, which roil, float

around, dissolve, or settle out in me.

~ JD

CXXVI.

O thou, my lovely boy, who in thy power

Dost hold Time's fickle glass, his sickle, hour;

Who hast by waning grown, and therein show'st

Thy lovers withering as thy sweet self grow'st;

If Nature, sovereign mistress over wrack,

As thou goest onwards, still will pluck thee back,

She keeps thee to this purpose, that her skill

May time disgrace and wretched minutes kill.

Yet fear her, O thou minion of her pleasure!

She may detain, but not still keep, her treasure:

Her audit, though delay'd, answer'd must be,

And her quietus is to render thee.

~ WS

126.

'7734 53507 808327338
'577345 3507 5663 35006
'55178 3507 53751
'7105 3507 57714
'805 50804 '5376608 55178 5,3773516
'32008 604 535508 218045
'(73817) 537818 37816377! 7735 5304 35380

'53160 7002 06 05
--53504 + 53504 '53504 + 53704 '53704 + 53704
'32135 + 335 5338 + 35336

'304 5,345 :018 '''577345-335 57735 345

'577345-018
--57718 345 '54615 345 '53145 345
'53!7 34 '46!4 5,34 '5306 34
'5376616 345 (¿53722!5 345)
'53200 34 '58008 532135 34
'53553580 345 '53760 34
'53704 + '58008 '5637 7735 5304 37816173

'1 + '345 '34--31738 (¿53160 7018) 5063
'50607 3507 57!615
'53705 3507 53045
'3718 3507 5317738
'37816377! 5! 50607 04
'50607 32160 7018 53704-08237 35007

~ JD

CXXVII.

In the old age black was not counted fair,

Or if it were, it bore not beauty's name;

But now is black beauty's successive heir,

And beauty slander'd with a bastard shame:

For since each hand hath put on nature's power,

Fairing the foul with art's false borrow'd face,

Sweet beauty hath no name, no holy bower,

But is profaned, if not lives in disgrace.

Therefore my mistress' brows are raven black,

Her eyes so suited, and they mourners seem

At such who, not born fair, no beauty lack,

Slandering creation with a false esteem:

Yet so they mourn, becoming of their woe,

That every tongue says beauty should look so.

~ WS

127.

should I compare you to a summer day?

now why would i do that, you little whore?

you know your cards, but you don't know the play.

you've got a shell, but you forgot the core.

you're hot. it's true. you burn with borrowed heat.

your body's a ridiculous façade.

you resonate with everything you meet,

& stress just gets your panties in a wad.

you stupid drama queen! forget yourself!

your fucking self-absorption is a waste!

your life's hijacked by everybody else!

you have too much to lose to know your place.

forget your ears & listen to my voice.

my silences outsuit your petty noise.

~ JD

CXXVIII.

How oft, when thou, my music, music play'st,

Upon that blessed wood whose motion sounds

With thy sweet fingers, when thou gently sway'st

The wiry concord that mine ear confounds,

Do I envy those jacks that nimble leap

To kiss the tender inward of thy hand,

Whilst my poor lips, which should that harvest reap,

At the wood's boldness by thee blushing stand!

To be so tickled, they would change their state

And situation with those dancing chips,

O'er whom thy fingers walk with gentle gait,

Making dead wood more blest than living lips.

Since saucy jacks so happy are in this,

Give them thy fingers, me thy lips to kiss.

~ WS

128.

the words you use show where you're coming from.

simplicity and genuine disjuncts

reveal just how your universe can hum...

...unless, because of me, you're in a funk.

i've heard your guard-dogs barking, each to each.

i know your golden gates are guarded well.

but look! i come with gifts & dripping feet,

beneath which flowers bloom, beneath their spell.

i ooze with sweat and aloe, and with spring.

i bear no teeth, no fangs, no sword, no stick.

my open hands will be enough to bring

to dogs & women: pure love & justice.

so bare your heart to me, my love, my soul,

and let all of my parts remake your whole.

~ JD

CXXIX.

The expense of spirit in a waste of shame

Is lust in action; and till action, lust

Is perjured, murderous, bloody, full of blame,

Savage, extreme, rude, cruel, not to trust,

Enjoy'd no sooner but despised straight,

Past reason hunted, and no sooner had

Past reason hated, as a swallow'd bait

On purpose laid to make the taker mad;

Mad in pursuit and in possession so;

Had, having, and in quest to have, extreme;

A bliss in proof, and proved, a very woe;

Before, a joy proposed; behind, a dream.

All this the world well knows; yet none knows well

To shun the heaven that leads men to this hell.

~ WS

129.

CXXX.

My mistress' eyes are nothing like the sun;

Coral is far more red than her lips' red;

If snow be white, why then her breasts are dun;

If hairs be wires, black wires grow on her head.

I have seen roses damask'd, red and white,

But no such roses see I in her cheeks;

And in some perfumes is there more delight

Than in the breath that from my mistress reeks.

I love to hear her speak, yet well I know

That music hath a far more pleasing sound;

I grant I never saw a goddess go;

My mistress, when she walks, treads on the ground:

And yet, by heaven, I think my love as rare

As any she belied with false compare.

~ WS

130.

the cover always permeates the page,

whose X it intimates in i's & t's.

an exit and an entrance and a stage:

its weapons pierce. its genitalia please.

it only wears a mask to advertise.

subtitles, fabrics, paints, & registers:

coordinated for beholders' eyes...

...wombs, snakes, or apples...or prime ministers.

divert, digress, decay, & decompose?

a pattern here becomes a pattern there.

allegiances exceed the first few rows,

like proverbs dressed in period underwear.

so sit, my love, and sing me all your book:

until my heart has nowhere else to look.

~ JD

CXXXI.

Thou art as tyrannous, so as thou art,

As those whose beauties proudly make them cruel;

For well thou know'st to my dear doting heart

Thou art the fairest and most precious jewel.

Yet, in good faith, some say that thee behold

Thy face hath not the power to make love groan:

To say they err I dare not be so bold,

Although I swear it to myself alone.

And, to be sure that is not false I swear,

A thousand groans, but thinking on thy face,

One on another's neck, do witness bear

Thy black is fairest in my judgment's place.

In nothing art thou black save in thy deeds,

And thence this slander, as I think, proceeds.

~ WS

131.

when you have called on all your other gods
and they can't save you from the wild boars;
when darkness falls on all your cones and rods
and oceans find your boat without its oars;

or when, perchance, some rival should emerge
and wing your lusty soul up to the sun,
to fill its every want, desire, and urge...
...& as you fall, you realize *you're undone*—

then call my name, and through the winds of time,
that clarion shall cause my soul to stir;
and in a blink you will recall that i'm
the only one who loves you forever.

but don't call me to your dainty little
ha-ha sessions with me in the middle.

~ JD

CXXXII.

Thine eyes I love, and they, as pitying me,

Knowing thy heart torments me with disdain,

Have put on black and loving mourners be,

Looking with pretty ruth upon my pain.

And truly not the morning sun of heaven

Better becomes the grey cheeks of the east,

Nor that full star that ushers in the even

Doth half that glory to the sober west,

As those two mourning eyes become thy face:

O, let it then as well beseem thy heart

To mourn for me, since mourning doth thee grace,

And suit thy pity like in every part.

Then will I swear beauty herself is black

And all they foul that thy complexion lack.

~ WS

132.

disperse the fogs of unreality,

the clouds of doubt, the mists of the mundane,

who shroud instinct in impropriety,

whose fears have blurred *acceptance* into *sane*.

revise your habits. change your stratagems.

remind your neck of frets it never plays.

go tell your beggars you're not mad at them.

sing to your skies and dance to better days.

but don't sit there and tell me i'm a rock

whose metamorphoses are far too slow

to keep the beat of your internal clock

unless your skies are falling, snow on snow.

and do not dare my soul into your eyes

until your summer suns have cleared their skies.

~ JD

VII

CXXXIII.

Beshrew that heart that makes my heart to groan

For that deep wound it gives my friend and me!

Is't not enough to torture me alone,

But slave to slavery my sweet'st friend must be?

Me from myself thy cruel eye hath taken,

And my next self thou harder hast engross'd:

Of him, myself, and thee, I am forsaken;

A torment thrice threefold thus to be cross'd.

Prison my heart in thy steel bosom's ward,

But then my friend's heart let my poor heart bail;

Whoe'er keeps me, let my heart be his guard;

Thou canst not then use rigor in my gaol:

And yet thou wilt; for I, being pent in thee,

Perforce am thine, and all that is in me.

~ WS

133.

if everyone remembered everything,

then cosmic forces would befall us all.

selection is the conscience of the king.

the females are too short. the men too tall.

beware the power of omnipotence.

the GENOME standing ready at the door.

intelligence provides a poor defense

for lust & greed & other names for *more*...

...*insanity* does not provide a plea

to cosmic juries who recall the day

when spores & sparrows, dinosaurs & fleas

remembered everything necessary.

and who are you, oh *homo sapiens*,

who claim your *knowledge*, who should claim your *ends*?

~ JD

CXXXIV.

So, now I have confess'd that he is thine,

And I myself am mortgaged to thy will,

Myself I'll forfeit, so that other mine

Thou wilt restore, to be my comfort still:

But thou wilt not, nor he will not be free,

For thou art covetous and he is kind;

He learn'd but surety-like to write for me

Under that bond that him as fast doth bind.

The statute of thy beauty thou wilt take,

Thou usurer, that put'st forth all to use,

And sue a friend came debtor for my sake;

So him I lose through my unkind abuse.

Him have I lost; thou hast both him and me:

He pays the whole, and yet am I not free.

~ WS

134.

my time on earth has flown invisible

& supersonic through what air? what skies?

my weight approaches zed-divisible

and my estate, once solid, rarifies.

i watch my opulence evaporate.

my truest friends, the ghosts of yesteryear,

now mill around my house & buy my plates.

my flesh & my companions disappear.

naked i came & bloody & screaming...

and now my memories, blood-let, soak the ground.

the highest bidder's paddle buys my meaning.

my organs sell for pennies on the pound.

the bowl is broken and the cord undone.

i sell my soul to buy oblivion.

~ JD

CXXXV.

Whoever hath her wish, thou hast thy 'Will,'

And 'Will' to boot, and 'Will' in overplus;

More than enough am I that vex thee still,

To thy sweet will making addition thus.

Wilt thou, whose will is large and spacious,

Not once vouchsafe to hide my will in thine?

Shall will in others seem right gracious,

And in my will no fair acceptance shine?

The sea all water, yet receives rain still

And in abundance addeth to his store;

So thou, being rich in 'Will,' add to thy 'Will'

One will of mine, to make thy large 'Will' more.

Let no unkind, no fair beseechers kill;

Think all but one, and me in that one 'Will.'

~ WS

135.

Though I beseech, you'll have your morning "Jole."

If tired, your "Jole" is roughened till he rise;

If jolly, then you duplicate your goal—

With "Jole" you twice effect your carnal prize.

If this were not enough, on afternoons

You'll have another "Jole" or two or three.

Your appetite to thrust, to jole balloons:

At dinner you command your "Jole" of me.

Transport my ship-wrecked body to the bed

Then lash it to the frame and play at roles

With tempest-"Jole" your climax comes to head

(you aim to mount the nastiest of "Joles.")

Your boundless vigor takes its daily toll—

You cradle and prepare tomorrow's "Jole."

~ JD

CXXXVI.

If thy soul cheque thee that I come so near,

Swear to thy blind soul that I was thy 'Will,'

And will, thy soul knows, is admitted there;

Thus far for love my love-suit, sweet, fulfil.

'Will' will fulfil the treasure of thy love,

Ay, fill it full with wills, and my will one.

In things of great receipt with ease we prove

Among a number one is reckon'd none:

Then in the number let me pass untold,

Though in thy stores' account I one must be;

For nothing hold me, so it please thee hold

That nothing me, a something sweet to thee:

Make but my name thy love, and love that still,

And then thou lovest me, for my name is 'Will.'

~ WS

136.

if ever i loved, i loved life. if ev-
er i die, i'll die for love. dare i live
forever droll, devoid of deed, devoid
of role? i roil, a flood of fevered love.

i flare, a jovial, fire-fed la-
va of life. "eve died of a dead idea,"
all dildo-fed ova jeer. a fool for
love, i fill a void: i, jove, do delve for ore.

i dive, i jive, i rove, arrive, a veiled,
a florid ode: relieved of drivel, fer-
al, rife, i revel over all of life.
i live life real: a flavorade ideal,

a dollar-raider, idol-defiler,
vivid fiddler...jaded devil of lore.

CXXXVII.

Thou blind fool, Love, what dost thou to mine eyes,

That they behold, and see not what they see?

They know what beauty is, see where it lies,

Yet what the best is take the worst to be.

If eyes corrupt by over-partial looks

Be anchor'd in the bay where all men ride,

Why of eyes' falsehood hast thou forged hooks,

Whereto the judgment of my heart is tied?

Why should my heart think that a several plot

Which my heart knows the wide world's common place?

Or mine eyes seeing this, say this is not,

To put fair truth upon so foul a face?

In things right true my heart and eyes have erred,

And to this false plague are they now transferr'd.

~ WS

137.

desire's irony is that it hides

from the prying eyes of the question, "WHY?"

what "turns you on?" men? women? boyfriends? brides?

(who decides?) dicks? boobs? assholes? legs? vagi-

nas? (WHY?) rough sex or tantra? fingernails

or earlobes? nerve-bundles play their roles, it's

true... but what about you? the sex-symbols

that you adopt transform your images.

the psycho-code of your pleasure-programs,

adapting language-figures from your tribe,

becomes your dialect & idioms,

the way you speak sexual English. (WHY?)

next time you say, "nice shoes! so...wanna fuck?"

ask, "do my lusts come from *choice* or *luck*?"

~ JD

CXXXVIII.

When my love swears that she is made of truth

I do believe her, though I know she lies,

That she might think me some untutor'd youth,

Unlearned in the world's false subtleties.

Thus vainly thinking that she thinks me young,

Although she knows my days are past the best,

Simply I credit her false speaking tongue:

On both sides thus is simple truth suppress'd.

But wherefore says she not she is unjust?

And wherefore say not I that I am old?

O, love's best habit is in seeming trust,

And age in love loves not to have years told:

Therefore I lie with her and she with me,

And in our faults by lies we flatter'd be.

~ WS

138.

i will not thank you for your flattery,

or genuflect to merit your embrace,

transform myself to your commodity,

or think myself in your objective case.

you're worse than narcissus. you're self-absorbed,

but need to feel yourself objectified...

so doting eyes & minds become your mirrors.

you wear their stares. their smiles are where you hide.

their language is the fun-house of your being,

the circus where you host your self-esteem,

retreat into the safety of a thing—

a coin, an accolade, a ghost, a dream.

your prowess and your praise fail to impress.

go elsewhere with your frail false-consciousness.

~ JD

CXXXIX.

O, call not me to justify the wrong

That thy unkindness lays upon my heart;

Wound me not with thine eye but with thy tongue;

Use power with power and slay me not by art.

Tell me thou lovest elsewhere, but in my sight,

Dear heart, forbear to glance thine eye aside:

What need'st thou wound with cunning when thy might

Is more than my o'er-press'd defense can bide?

Let me excuse thee: ah! my love well knows

Her pretty looks have been mine enemies,

And therefore from my face she turns my foes,

That they elsewhere might dart their injuries:

Yet do not so; but since I am near slain,

Kill me outright with looks and rid my pain.

~ WS

139.

separate and equal, let us live our lives,

as independent but dependable;

when in disgrace with fortune and men's eyes,

to find each other indispensable.

but do not let this parting of the ways

become the premise of some deeper woe;

and do not cease to hope for better days,

when hand in hand again we two might go.

but let the bitter taste of this reprieve

prepare your palate for my sweet return.

i went in black when it was time to leave,

but dawn brings every balanced hue to burn.

till then, my love, my heart, my world is spent

to bring conclusion to our argument.

~ JD

CXL.

Be wise as thou art cruel; do not press

My tongue-tied patience with too much disdain;

Lest sorrow lend me words and words express

The manner of my pity-wanting pain.

If I might teach thee wit, better it were,

Though not to love, yet, love, to tell me so;

As testy sick men, when their deaths be near,

No news but health from their physicians know;

For if I should despair, I should grow mad,

And in my madness might speak ill of thee:

Now this ill-wresting world is grown so bad,

Mad slanderers by mad ears believed be,

That I may not be so, nor thou belied,

Bear thine eyes straight, though thy proud heart go wide.

~ WS

140.

i walk among symbols & figures & signs.

i watch their fine, divine, amorphous forms

define what's mine, transform my mind, & style

abnormal metaphors for me. i'm torn

between god-complexes & word-complexes,

neuroses, psychoses, & distorted ego-

emanations; born to battle both sexes

without taking sides, since every word i know

refers to me. yes, you heard me right. i

just called myself tupac. and dasein. and

sappho. and ice cream. and fuck if you can

tell the difference. i'm not insane. are you?

take all your words and supplement them with:

myth comes from life and life: comes from myth.

~ JD

CXLI.

In faith, I do not love thee with mine eyes,

For they in thee a thousand errors note;

But 'tis my heart that loves what they despise,

Who in despite of view is pleased to dote;

Nor are mine ears with thy tongue's tune delighted,

Nor tender feeling, to base touches prone,

Nor taste, nor smell, desire to be invited

To any sensual feast with thee alone:

But my five wits nor my five senses can

Dissuade one foolish heart from serving thee,

Who leaves unsway'd the likeness of a man,

Thy proud hearts slave and vassal wretch to be:

Only my plague thus far I count my gain,

That she that makes me sin awards me pain.

~ WS

141.

as wasps & orchids draw themselves along,

with nothing left to lose save how guitars,

untempered through the tempest, string their songs—

for embers that die faster than their stars;

as advertisements perlocute their wares,

& time & tide make heartbeats do their best;

as blood & rust & death find unprepared

the cards that are held closest to the vest—

a soul within constraints is still a soul.

the body is the will's sommelier.

the spirit thrives through obstacles & goals,

the power of the mind, through work & play...

...environments & dna & lust

create this universe of fear & trust.

~ JD

CXLII.

Love is my sin and thy dear virtue hate,

Hate of my sin, grounded on sinful loving:

O, but with mine compare thou thine own state,

And thou shalt find it merits not reproving;

Or, if it do, not from those lips of thine,

That have profaned their scarlet ornaments

And seal'd false bonds of love as oft as mine,

Robb'd others' beds' revenues of their rents.

Be it lawful I love thee, as thou lovest those

Whom thine eyes woo as mine importune thee:

Root pity in thy heart, that when it grows

Thy pity may deserve to pitied be.

If thou dost seek to have what thou dost hide,

By self-example mayst thou be denied!

~ WS

142.

they say you never get a second chance

to make a first impression on yourself.

the social mirror shows: a psychophant.

to live for self: to live for someone else.

the arbor of my figments is your world.

the ardor of my arms is your embrace.

the grove of our encampments: boy & girl.

and armored limbs befit the human race.

so court your life of shielded novelty—

whose fruits your bed enjoys at my expense.

unseen, unminded: our monogamy.

a past forgotten for a present tense.

reflect a bit before you slight my trust,

and trade my lasting love for fleeting lust.

~ JD

CXLIII.

Lo! as a careful housewife runs to catch
One of her feather'd creatures broke away,
Sets down her babe and makes an swift dispatch
In pursuit of the thing she would have stay,

Whilst her neglected child holds her in chase,
Cries to catch her whose busy care is bent
To follow that which flies before her face,
Not prizing her poor infant's discontent;

So runn'st thou after that which flies from thee,
Whilst I thy babe chase thee afar behind;
But if thou catch thy hope, turn back to me,
And play the mother's part, kiss me, be kind:

So will I pray that thou mayst have thy 'Will,'
If thou turn back, and my loud crying still.

~ WS

143.

i scream my way into maturity—
my lungs must learn to drink your alien air.
this violent birth to insecurity—
& i still can't survive without your care.

you bring me bruised & bloody to this place.
our cord of codependence has been cut.
my open eyes this independence day
can see our severed symbiotic trust.

is this because i kicked? is this your spite?
this cosmic hell of liberty & choice?
chaotic kicks & flails are my new rights,
the raging impotence of this new voice.

new love, sincere, sadistic, in your eyes
looks down on me & smiles as i cry.

~ JD

CXLIV.

Two loves I have of comfort and despair,

Which like two spirits do suggest me still:

The better angel is a man right fair,

The worser spirit a woman colour'd ill.

To win me soon to hell, my female evil

Tempteth my better angel from my side,

And would corrupt my saint to be a devil,

Wooing his purity with her foul pride.

And whether that my angel be turn'd fiend

Suspect I may, but not directly tell;

But being both from me, both to each friend,

I guess one angel in another's hell:

Yet this shall I ne'er know, but live in doubt,

Till my bad angel fire my good one out.

~ WS

144.

our fears are best addressed as embryos—

before the helix starts unraveling,

before the table's set, before our foes—

our faith & fate turn out our gods & kings.

the father must be fierce and reticent,

the mother & the child be warmed and fed.

assailants must be battled, life be spent;

both plant & meat spied out and harvested.

the shelters that churn out philosophy

have borne these instincts far in human sight.

alone, we fear. united, we believe.

we know. we fight. we win. respect makes right.

the best gestations make the greatest lives:

our zen, instinct, & power make us wise.

~ JD

CXLV.

Those lips that Love's own hand did make
Breathed forth the sound that said 'I hate'
To me that languish'd for her sake;
But when she saw my woeful state,

Straight in her heart did mercy come,
Chiding that tongue that ever sweet
Was used in giving gentle doom,
And taught it thus anew to greet:

'I hate' she alter'd with an end,
That follow'd it as gentle day
Doth follow night, who like a fiend
From heaven to hell is flown away;

'I hate' from hate away she threw,
And saved my life, saying 'not you.'

~ WS

145.

...Head, Heart and Gut are passing *wine,*

till all *divine* that it's the *time* to talk.

(the *syncopations* and the *rhymes*

are slanted like *bluegrass*...)

...till Knowledge, Love, and Instinct come

into the room, where each is recognized

by: *SAME ATTRACTED TO THE S◉ME!*

and so, to bed, six gods and goddESSEs...

...but *Styx*, forever jealous, *screams*!

(and so imposing is this Lord of Earth

on: "[a] one! [and a] two! [and a] *Being!*")

that *Strife* (disguised *as Hatred*) *slips on in*...

...¡¡¡ *Love/Hate!!!* is born (& *hides in*: "It Depends!")

(...all gods are *means* when life has found its *ends*...)

CXLVI.

Poor soul, the centre of my sinful earth,

[Feeding] these rebel powers that thee array;

Why dost thou pine within and suffer dearth,

Painting thy outward walls so costly gay?

Why so large cost, having so short a lease,

Dost thou upon thy fading mansion spend?

Shall worms, inheritors of this excess,

Eat up thy charge? is this thy body's end?

Then soul, live thou upon thy servant's loss,

And let that pine to aggravate thy store;

Buy terms divine in selling hours of dross;

Within be fed, without be rich no more:

So shalt thou feed on Death, that feeds on men,

And Death once dead, there's no more dying then.

~ WS

146.

a thunder rumbles under etna's mound.
some ancient son of heaven shifts his bulk
& heaves his hulking mass. what once were grounds
for buried gods behold their heroes skulk

off grumbling, nursing mortal wounds. these one-
time titans turn to factoid-dots we plot
on scientific seismographs. but soon
they may return. for earth recalls the hot

millennia when (not so long ago)
the molten lava burst her crust, and flowed
past naught but lifeless rocks. if this be so,
o humankind, tread lightly as ye go.

for just below a vulcan fury lurks
to purge from earth this world of human works.

~ JD

CXLVII.

My love is as a fever, longing still

For that which longer nurseth the disease,

Feeding on that which doth preserve the ill,

The uncertain sickly appetite to please.

My reason, the physician to my love,

Angry that his prescriptions are not kept,

Hath left me, and I desperate now approve

Desire is death, which physic did except.

Past cure I am, now reason is past care,

And frantic-mad with evermore unrest;

My thoughts and my discourse as madmen's are,

At random from the truth vainly express'd;

For I have sworn thee fair and thought thee bright,

Who art as black as hell, as dark as night.

~ WS

147.

your absence is my fever: steely sky,

pale vivid sunlight, mercury rising

in my veins forever; constant ring-

ing in my ears; dull numbness in my

limbs & tongue; faint omnipresent acid scent.

in this frenzied state i forget togeth-

erness—how i (sans flu) felt you or wheth-

er my moistened buds intruded you. did

it happen? ...this chasm, lethe, styx, turns

all to one pain-puree: day blends to day.

all wears & tears & sweat & blood;

all wares & tares & wheat & mud;

all where's & there's & good & bad

swirl in this void between us, girl.

~ JD

CXLVIII.

O me, what eyes hath Love put in my head,

Which have no correspondence with true sight!

Or, if they have, where is my judgment fled,

That censures falsely what they see aright?

If that be fair whereon my false eyes dote,

What means the world to say it is not so?

If it be not, then love doth well denote

Love's eye is not so true as all men's 'No.'

How can it? O, how can Love's eye be true,

That is so vex'd with watching and with tears?

No marvel then, though I mistake my view;

The sun itself sees not till heaven clears.

O cunning Love! with tears thou keep'st me blind,

Lest eyes well-seeing thy foul faults should find.

~ WS

148.

to go where there is wisdom on the wind,

where solitude brings forth its ripest fruits,

& no communion's ever called a sin,

& lips that burn with words are never mute;

to walk where self-expression is the rule,

& dance unshackled from your self-regret;

to sing to victory your cosmic duels,

& love the only universe you've met—

destroy the menacing panopticon,

the phantom eyes that ogle you to death,

the evil host whose ghosts make you their pawn,

the mournful *shoulds* that measure every breath...

...breathe in the only air you'll ever know

to overcome the world you undergo.

~ JD

CXLIX.

Canst thou, O cruel! say I love thee not,

When I against myself with thee partake?

Do I not think on thee, when I forgot

Am of myself, all tyrant, for thy sake?

Who hateth thee that I do call my friend?

On whom frown'st thou that I do fawn upon?

Nay, if thou lour'st on me, do I not spend

Revenge upon myself with present moan?

What merit do I in myself respect,

That is so proud thy service to despise,

When all my best doth worship thy defect,

Commanded by the motion of thine eyes?

But, love, hate on, for now I know thy mind;

Those that can see thou lovest, and I am blind.

~ WS

149.

at eventide, the feral fauna frolic

on the thoroughfare, until the headlights,

blind with rage, unleash their fury, scorned

& feminine. now mangled & forlorn,

with foaming mouths, their glassy eyes become

their last appeal. a baby dies of hunger

in the night. a house-cat fondly

reminisces on its owner from between

the bloody teeth of wild dogs. these are

the eyes of the question that quaver

between the summer love of soft hearts & hard

winter's need to dominate. the world has

few tyrants & fewer vegetarians,

& none that protest mass insecticide.

~ JD

CL.

O, from what power hast thou this powerful might

With insufficiency my heart to sway?

To make me give the lie to my true sight,

And swear that brightness doth not grace the day?

Whence hast thou this becoming of things ill,

That in the very refuse of thy deeds

There is such strength and warrantize of skill

That, in my mind, thy worst all best exceeds?

Who taught thee how to make me love thee more

The more I hear and see just cause of hate?

O, though I love what others do abhor,

With others thou shouldst not abhor my state:

If thy unworthiness raised love in me,

More worthy I to be beloved of thee.

~ WS

150.

each species has its featured deities—

ponderous gestalts intuited by squirts

of enzymes; cytoplasmic mentalese,

societies that hunt, digest and flirt.

life sprung from hell's reducing atmosphere.

the atoms of the first planarians

knew well the feel of hormones making fear.

dolphins have fins and proletarians.

so you, sweet goddess of my dopamine:

you shall not go without your parthenon.

your mystic rule of my endorphins means

your primal place in my heart's pantheon.

each breath i take you are my *corps d'esprit*:

homo mensura deae homini.

~ JD

CLI.

Love is too young to know what conscience is;

Yet who knows not conscience is born of love?

Then, gentle cheater, urge not my amiss,

Lest guilty of my faults thy sweet self prove:

For, thou betraying me, I do betray

My nobler part to my gross body's treason;

My soul doth tell my body that he may

Triumph in love; flesh stays no father reason;

But, rising at thy name, doth point out thee

As his triumphant prize. Proud of this pride,

He is contented thy poor drudge to be,

To stand in thy affairs, fall by thy side.

No want of conscience hold it that I call

Her 'love' for whose dear love I rise and fall.

~ WS

151.

conscience is born of love, where love is free—

a love beyond the lust to own and have.

the measure i have used must measure me—

i will not be your master or your slave.

my love, you bear my conscience every day.

to you and to myself i must be true.

i feel no guilt except when I have made

you sad, or broken promises to you.

as earth knows life, our conscience is conceived.

our bodies form this fair, good, living bond.

but being-unto-death, my will-to-live

erupts beyond the pale of right and wrong.

my joy and pain: to love you in my flesh;

to know you and be known: my happiness.

~ JD

CLII.

In loving thee thou know'st I am forsworn,

But thou art twice forsworn, to me love swearing,

In act thy bed-vow broke and new faith torn,

In vowing new hate after new love bearing.

But why of two oaths' breach do I accuse thee,

When I break twenty? I am perjured most;

For all my vows are oaths but to misuse thee

And all my honest faith in thee is lost,

For I have sworn deep oaths of thy deep kindness,

Oaths of thy love, thy truth, thy constancy,

And, to enlighten thee, gave eyes to blindness,

Or made them swear against the thing they see;

For I have sworn thee fair; more perjured I,

To swear against the truth so foul a lie!

~ WS

152.

I guess this is goodbye, my goddess-girl.

Goodbye my wholesome good, my general evil.

My nymph, your naughty virtue rocked my world,

I was your god in love, your beast, your devil.

Although I'm left to idiolatry,

My day does not reproach you for your night—

Your fuck was not an infidelity—

A goddess eats when she has appetite.

So does a bitch – and strung between the two,

You walk your rope of impropriety.

The untamed dogs of your mind's desire do

Whatever they want, outside society.

My Venus, all is fair in love and war.

Always your man, your god, your devil—Mars.

CLIII.

Cupid laid by his brand, and fell asleep:
A maid of Dian's this advantage found,
And his love-kindling fire did quickly steep
In a cold valley-fountain of that ground;

Which borrow'd from this holy fire of Love
A dateless lively heat, still to endure,
And grew a seething bath, which yet men prove
Against strange maladies a sovereign cure.

But at my mistress' eye Love's brand new-fired,
The boy for trial needs would touch my breast;
I, sick withal, the help of bath desired,
And thither hied, a sad distemper'd guest,

But found no cure: the bath for my help lies
Where Cupid got new fire—my mistress' eyes.

~ WS

153.

I, Cupid, pricked myself with my own brand,

And yearned to ravish Psyche's purest frame.

(Mindless I'd been aroused by my own hand),

I came unseen, by night, to quench my flame.

But Psyche, not content with dreamy Lust,

By candle brought to light my hidden truth.

Then I awoke, enraged at her distrust,

Since sight of me was Mind's forbidden fruit.

O Psyche, too naïve to view my form!

Your gaze was still your quest to "have" in mind

A trophy-image for your memory's store!

To have is human. Loving is divine.

So now I rule your drives and wander free.

You serve your idols & ideas of me.

~ JD

CLIV.

The little Love-god lying once asleep

Laid by his side his heart-inflaming brand,

Whilst many nymphs that vow'd chaste life to keep

Came tripping by; but in her maiden hand

The fairest votary took up that fire

Which many legions of true hearts had warm'd;

And so the general of hot desire

Was sleeping by a virgin hand disarm'd.

This brand she quenched in a cool well by,

Which from Love's fire took heat perpetual,

Growing a bath and healthful remedy

For men diseased; but I, my mistress' thrall,

Came there for cure, and this by that I prove,

Love's fire heats water, water cools not love.

~ WS

154.

i,
id,
aid
said
ideas
as i die.
i, *dasein*,
wade in "is."
i wane as id.
i die as want.
i wait and see.
i warn & tease id-
deities - warn as
dna. i resist a new
satire. ears widen.
fears side in water,
terrae, winds, & fire, as
dies irae strewn afar.
fantasie-carriers wed.
darwin is after a secret:
id-fiats create new rears.
scarred entities fear war.
id fares erotic warrantees,
as reference is a word's trait.
war, frost & fate race in desires.
if, afterwards, erections arise
in orifices, afterward, reassert:
"i, dasein-waters, refract eros' fire."
reason retires, rewired as traffic.
renewed, i first react as fears or ire.
i, eros, re-write *différance* as "arrests."
i, *esse*, transfer "we" for "i"... & re-trace id-arcs.
terse answers fire our artifice. sacred
dice create. warriors refine fate's ruses,
since fate creates & mirrors us if we re-read:
"from fairest creatures we desire increase."

~ JD

notes

Sonnet 1: Traditionally, the first 126 sonnets in Shakespeare's collection are thought to form a unit, addressed to the "Fair Youth," a younger male friend of Shakespeare's, Platonic or possibly otherwise (cf. sonnet 20). Each reader interpolates his or her own version of love, respect, friendship and sex into the interstices of each text. Dominant Western values have had over 400 years to establish a reading tradition for Shakespeare's sonnets. Here, as elsewhere, that can make Shakespeare sound a bit rapey. Or perhaps Shakespeare is merely accustomed to an unconventionally honest battle of powerful wills. "Rosebud" is an allusion to the film, *Citizen Kane*.

Sonnet 2: This sonnet is an allusion to Genesis 35, the relationship between Jacob and Rachel and the birth of Benjamin. In question is heavenly versus earthly hope, couched in scathing irony toward the presumptiveness of patriarchal lineage.

Sonnet 3: This sonnet's imagery reflects the myth of Narcissus (cf. Ovid, *Metamorphoses*, book 3) as well as the "orgasm as death" motif of Elizabethan times. The juxtaposition of mirror imagery and procreation is interesting in light of Lacan's suggestion that mirrors/self-reflection are crucial to ego-formation, and in light of the importance of "the mirror test" in assessing the self-awareness of species. Mirror imagery pervades my sonnets.

Sonnet 4: The myth of Tantalus is used here as a symbol of the fleetingness of material possession. The paradox of "one hand paying the other" resonates with themes of self-reference that permeate my sonnets.

Sonnet 5: Themes of the seasons, water, death, beauty, and reproduction blend in these first few sonnets (both mine and Shakespeare's.) My response may be read as a critique of Ego in Shakespeare's appeals to the Fair Youth.

Sonnet 6: Connecting sonnets 5 and 6 (as indeed Shakespeare does), I illuminate themes of chaos, madness, and chance as a counterpoint to Shakespeare, who favors identity, reason, and choice. Allusion to the myth of Pandora's box.

Sonnet 7: Engaging the logic of Shakespeare's sonnet, I turn the tables and use Shakespeare's own premises to arrive at the opposite of his conclusion. Marxist allusions.

Sonnet 8: Themes of chaos translate into musical metaphors in this sonnet.

Sonnet 9: Shakespeare's "widow" transforms into a black widow spider.

Sonnet 10: Shame and suicide. Self-esteem and self-concept. Shakespeare had some quite clever logic here. Still, rather dark.

Sonnet 11: Against Social Darwinism...at least on the level of the individual. Psychoanalytic lack.

Sonnet 12: This sonnet opens with an allusion to Eliot's, "I have measured out my life with coffee spoons." Images of bride and whore may be read against John's *Apocalypse*.

Sonnet 13: Allusion to the "Butterfly Effect" of physics. Challenge to the shallowness of human labels (cf. Nietzsche, *On Truth and Lying in an Extramoral Sense*).

Sonnet 14: Sound poem. Imagery poem. Astrology allusions to Pisces (hence Aphrodite and Eros). "Oikos" is Greek for "house." There are 12 chromatic tones and 12 signs. Introduces numerology theme.

Sonnet 15: Ecological poem. Altair (eagle) and Cygnus (swan) are summer constellations. Canis major (canine) and Taurus (bull) are winter constellations. A "when-when-then" sonnet - one of my favorite sonnet forms Shakespeare uses.

Sonnet 16: Inspired by e.e. cummings. Experimental. Gender wars poem. Many neologisms. "Parastigmatic" = "paradigm" + "stigma" (flower part, social disgrace). "Hemogoblins" = "hemoglobin" + "goblins." "Luminal" = "liminal" + "luminous." "Paradyxical" =

"paradoxical" + "parody." The last line is Latin: "Oh, that you would be willing to be changed by means of art into a memory."

Sonnet 17: Condensation of the traditional sonnet line from five feet into one. Iambic monometer.

Sonnet 18: The first "meta-sonnet." Here I've taken all the words of Shakespeare's sonnet and rearranged them into another sonnet. I've added a single word.

Sonnet 19: A logical turning of the tables. Closely follows the pace of Shakespeare's sonnet.

Sonnet 20: Experimental. The end of each line in the first stanza contains a palindrome. The French in line 4 reads, "Can you penetrate man, O bonobo?"

Sonnet 21: The German, "wie du eigentlich gewesen bist" echoes Leopold von Ranke's drive to make history scientific. It means "how you actually were."

Sonnet 22: If you love yourself at all, you're gay. I occasionally imagine "I, myself, and me" to be a more fecund psychoanalytic tool than Id, Ego, and Super-Ego.

Sonnet 23: Another "meta-sonnet." Opens with an abecedarius. In this sonnet, I've taken the letters in Shakespeare's sonnet and rearranged them into my own sonnet. It's not a perfect rearrangement (after all, I had to do the abecedarius)...but it is close.

Sonnet 24: The voice is that of a mirror talking to a canvas with a still life. Used as a metaphor for a relationship. "Tain" is a thin metallic foil used as backing for a mirror. First and last lines are word-level anagrams of each other.

Sonnet 25: The Latin, "semen scientiae sanguine fabri est," means "the blood of the workers is the seed of science."

Sonnet 26: The opening Latin means, "Oh mistress, speak and I will do what you desire. Do me, bitch! Harder! Yes!"

Sonnet 27: There's some deep, ancient etymology in this poem. Race, slavery, color. "All men are liars" becomes "all gods are liars."

Sonnet 28: A tip of the hat to Plato's Cave and Hedonism. Philosophical musings on existence, death, immortality, and Artificial Intelligence. In the blended space that emerges when one thinks my sonnet and Shakespeare's in one thought lies an existential caution for those whose hopes of Singularity are flavored only with optimism.

Sonnet 29: "William Shakespeare" is encoded in this sonnet. Reverberates with Psalm 29. Religionsgeschictlicheschule = 19th Century German textual criticism movement that treated religion under the rubric of history.

Sonnet 30: "Götzendämmerung" = German, "twilight of the idols" (cf. Nietzsche's work by this title). Influenced by Husserl's lectures on time consciousness. The last line is French, "in you, memory and time are completely lost." A tip of the hat to Proust.

Sonnet 31: Classical Marxist thought structures do no justice to the symbolic interweaving of gold (material) and ether (ideas) in this sonnet. Both flow.

Sonnet 32: Anagrams of the word "sonnets" in second line. "Sens" is French for "sense" and also "direction." "Mei nemo" is (somewhat strained) Latin for "my nobody," but also calls to mind the Greek "mnemo," for "memory." There are 154 sonnets in Shakespeare's collection, thus: 11 x 14 = 154. 154 is also encoded in the number of syllables in the sonnet.

Sonnet 33: Another number-play sonnet. Seven weekdays, seven diatonic notes. Cf. Nietzsche on health.

Sonnet 34: Acrostic. More number play: (12+10) x 7 = 154. Planets used to be called "wanderers," from which, "nomads."

Sonnet 35: Experimental. "Hetero orge" = Greek, "other anger." Tongue-in-cheek reference to "hetero or gay." "Homo mensura" = Latin, "Man is the measure." Ironically positioned next to "seize the dame," which recalls the English for the popular Latin phrase, "Carpe Diem." "Theorein" is Greek for thinking. Some palindromes. Venus de Milo. Chess metaphors.

Sonnet 36: This sonnet reads the same backward and forward. A "word-level" palindrome.

Sonnet 37: Ideas and blood. What does it mean for an idea (or meme) to be embodied? How do we do this for each other?

Sonnet 38: Inspired by Neruda. A poem to my Muse.

Sonnet 39: Questioning possession in relationships.

Sonnet 40: Overtly sexual.

Sonnet 41: Forces at play in relationships.

Sonnet 42: Neruda-inspired.

Sonnet 43: Core critique of representational theory of mind: socially and ethically absurd. Unavoidable?

Sonnet 44: "Fabula rasa" = Latin, "blank fable." A spin off the more common, "tabula rasa," "blank slate."

Sonnet 45: "Meta-sonnet." Here, I've taken the letters in each line of Shakespeare's sonnet and anagrammed them into the corresponding line of my own sonnet. So the letters in Shakespeare's Line 1 are the letters in my Line 1. I hint at this fact by repeating the word "anagram" in the poem. The French "sens" means "sense" but also "direction." "Ennui" means "boredom."

Sonnet 46: "Philosophy" combines the Greek words "love" and "wisdom."

Sonnet 47: Following Shakespeare, sonnet 47 is connected to sonnet 46. Themes of the distance between eye & heart, knowledge (mind) & love reverberate with Ovid's myth of *Cupid & Psyche*, and are reprised in my sonnets 153-154.

Sonnet 48: "Consumus ergo cogitamus" = Latin, "we are therefore we think," a reversal and socialization of the famous Cartesian dictum. "Terra incognita" = Latin, "unknown land."

Sonnet 49: Closely follows pace, flow, and internal structure of Shakespeare's sonnet.

Sonnet 50: Experimental. Inspired by Dickinson.

Sonnet 51: Myth of Icarus. Truth & language. Identity & love. "Tout-court" = French, "in short."

Sonnet 52: Philosophical commentary on conceptual and visceral pre-requisites for possession. "en toi hen mou" = Greek, "in you, my one."

Sonnet 53: Economic poem. The opening line is Latin, "what is your substance, fabricated one?" Echoes Marx, "Homo Faber," "man the maker." Adam Smith's "Invisible Hand" is also featured.

Sonnet 54: "Meta-sonnet." The entire sonnet rhymes with Shakespeare's sonnet.

Sonnet 55: Experimental form. Echoes Shakespeare's theme of Judgment Day.

Sonnet 56: Experimental. Picks up Shakespeare's themes of war, winter, and fate. Empedocles postulated four elements and two forces, love and strife.

Sonnet 57: Having versus being. "Also, ich habe hunger" = German, "I'm hungry." "Ho sete" = Italian, "I'm thirsty." Inspired in part by Heidegger.

Sonnet 58: Scathing ironic paraphrase of the logic of Shakespeare's sonnet.

Sonnet 59: Humans are computers metaphor.

Sonnet 60: Meditation on metamorphoses.

Sonnet 61: Subtle and subconscious.

Sonnet 62: Homage to the Janus, Narcissus, and Midas myths. Mirror imagery. Accordingly, palindromes throughout. "Mutandum" = Latin, "that which needs to be changed." "Sein" = German, "Being."

Sonnet 63: Experimental line breaks.

Sonnet 64: A historian's poem. The fall of Rome.

Sonnet 65: Code-interface: DNA and words.

Sonnet 66: Closely follows pace, flow and internal structure of Shakespeare's sonnet.

Sonnet 67: "Metasonnet." Line breaks of 8686 rhyme structure can be rearranged into a perfect sonnet. See what happens when you do.

Sonnet 68: Cf. Roland Barthes on "fashion statements."

Sonnet 69: Marxist theory of language inspired by the idea of "common" nouns. Cf. Jakobsen on paradigmatic and syntagmatic analysis. Cf. Heidegger for the idea that inspires "things thing." Cf. Leibniz on monads.

Sonnet 70: Questioning risk and being.

Sonnet 71: Identity and language. One of several allusions in the sonnets to Heidegger's famous remark, "Language is the house of Being." Levinas digs Freud here, substituting "Thou" for "Over-I" in the triad.

Sonnet 72: Here I've written a sonnet that rhymes with the digits of pi. 314159 becomes "dreams number us like pi." Poised at the synesthetic interface of the poetic and the mathematical, this sonnet opens the question of the meaning of repetition and reinforcement in either domain. Pi rhymes.

Sonnet 73: A somewhat cheeky take on what is actually a very nice sonnet by Shakespeare.

Sonnet 74: To paraphrase Heidegger, it's always someone else's death.

Sonnet 75: Aristotle called human beings "zoon politikon," "the political animal" (cf. "the social animal.") Zarathustra's cave is pregnant with symbolism in Nietzsche's work.

Sonnet 76: An ancient definition of human beings: two-footed and capable of laughter. This sonnet teems with double meanings. The meter changes performatively (from duodactylic to iambic) at the last couplet.

Sonnet 77: Mirror imagery at the midpoint of the sonnets. Self-references to palindromes, anagrams, and constrained poetry. Meta-poetic.

Sonnet 78: Overcoming fear. Last couplet foreshadows Sonnet 148.

Sonnet 79: Interface of code: DNA, letters, numbers. The line about translation foreshadows Sonnet 96.

Sonnet 80: Computer metaphor. Philosophy of language.

Sonnet 81: "William Shakespeare" is phonetically encoded in the opening to this sonnet.

Sonnet 82: Reflections on language and metaphor. Cf. Nietzsche, *On Truth and Lying*.

Sonnet 83: *Die Welt als Wille und Vorstellung* is the German title of a Schopenhauer work. The phrase in the sonnet means: "the world remains as will and representation." Ode to Samuel Beckett.

Sonnet 84: Experimental. Instead of 14 lines of 10 syllables each, the poem presents 10 lines of 14 syllables each. "I love you" is phonetically encoded.

Sonnet 85: "Commedia dell'arte" forms the mask-wearing, improvisational theme for this sonnet.

Sonnet 86: Meditation on death.

Sonnet 87: The Latin "si sentio, habeo ergo sum" means "if I am sentient, I have therefore I am," an ironic economic critique of Descartes. The French, "la vie: un rêve bref, un mot fini" means "life is a brief dream, a finished word." The Latin, "si somniat, homo in terra est," means "if he sleeps, the human being is in the earth."

Sonnet 88: Plato's Cave...as it relates to basic human sociability.

Sonnet 89: A sonnet for empowerment.

Sonnet 90: The opening line of this sonnet, in Aramaic, is famously one of the seven words of Christ at crucifixion. It means, "My god, my god, why have you forsaken me?" The phrase is partially replayed as an acrostic in the first letter of each line in this sonnet. Sonnet 90 also draws from Psalm 90 and Neruda's Sonnet 90 in his *Cien Sonetos de Amor*. This sonnet is rife with other literary allusions, including allusions to Aristotle / Nietzsche, Macbeth, Hamlet and Joseph

Conrad. The sonnet may be read as addressing a traditional deity or "the muse"—the latter reading foreshadowing sonnets 100-101.

Sonnet 91: A meditation on the sacred in the mundane.

Sonnet 92: Although light-hearted, this sonnet hints at some profound philosophical questions surrounding identity and chemistry.

Sonnet 93: Economic poem. Allusions to Genesis, Adam Smith, Plato's demiourgos, and Wall Street. Is all salience a delusion of reference?

Sonnet 94: Ode to Zizek and psychoanalysis. Cf. Deleuze & Foucault.

Sonnet 95: Tight with Shakespeare's logic. Homage to Hegel.

Sonnet 96: Recursion. A sonnet about the author writing sonnets in response to other sonnets. Appropriately, metaphor is invoked. Greek "metapherein" = carry-over, transference. Shakespeare repeats the final couplet from sonnet 36.

Sonnet 97: "Ex nihilo" = Latin, "out of nothing." Derrida references.

Sonnet 98: A sonnet that explores the difference between fucking and making love.

Sonnet 99: Ode to Chomsky, Jung and Crowley.

Sonnet 100: A reflection on death and immortality via the moment.

Sonnet 101: Another reflection on metaphor. One of my favorites.

Sonnet 102: Last Supper imagery.

Sonnet 103: John 1 imagery.

Sonnet 104: Economic poem.

Sonnet 105: Ode to Heraclitus and Heidegger.

Sonnet 106: On physical incarnation versus incarnation in art...a ubiquitous theme in Shakespeare's sonnets.

Sonnet 107: On death...as well as the interface between life on the page versus physical existence.

Sonnet 108: Experimental. Hint: first stanza should be read to include such words as "proscribed," "procreations," "circumvented," "circumlocutors," "contravened," "contradictions," "metaphysics" and "metaphors."

Sonnet 109: Experimental. Written from the perspective of an apex predator.

Sonnet 110: "Heraclitean" refers to "Heraclitus," Ancient Greek philosopher whose philosophy emphasized the impermanence of all things.

Sonnet 111: A love poem about overcoming insecurities. Star Wars allusions.

Sonnet 112: "Différance" is a French word borrowed from Jacques Derrida, meaning "difference" and "deferment." Torah story of Cain. Compare and contrast "They" to Heidegger's "Das Man." Nietzsche on pity, love, & herd morality.

Sonnet 113: On love, capitalism, and identity.

Sonnet 114: A philosophical study on the way that love knows.

Sonnet 115: Cf. Saul Williams.

Sonnet 116: A love poem. A howl of the soul. A sonnet exploring connection.

Sonnet 117: A lover's quarrel. *Fight Club* allusions.

Sonnet 118: More lover's quarrel.

Sonnet 119: A spin on Protagoras' "Homo Mensura," ("man is the measure"), "mensura homo" here means "the measure is the man."

Sonnet 120: A meditation on change over time and life in society.

Sonnet 121: Life in society, norms, and social judgment. Cf. Nietzsche, *On Truth and Lying.* "Friends of virtue" is an allusion to Aristotle's *Nicomachean Ethics*, Books 8-9. Gyges' ring is a mythical ring which affords invisibility at will (mentioned by Plato in *Republic*, Book 2). On "virtue" (ἀρετή), I recommend reading Aristotle through Nietzsche.

Sonnet 122: Computer metaphor.

Sonnet 123: Cf. Pythagoras. Whereas the voice in sonnet 115 was "time" or "life," the voice in sonnet 123 is "the future."

Sonnet 124: On poetry, life, and death. A love poem.

Sonnet 125: "Sum ergo volo" = Latin, "I am therefore I will."

Sonnet 126: Hint: turn the page upside down. *Ho logos* (ὁ λόγος) is a famously rich Ancient Greek term often translated as *word* or *reason*, but whose scope also includes such meanings as *account, computation, thinking* (as an inward debate of the soul), *formula, law, rule, hypothesis, plea, explanation, relation, correspondence, proportion, narrative, discussion, utterance,* or *topic.* It is the verbal noun form of the verb λέγω, to speak. Its descendants include our English *logic*, the *-ology* of our sciences, and our *lexicon.*

Sonnet 127: An allusion to Shakespeare's Sonnet 18. Encodes references to the card game poker in the last six lines.

Sonnet 128: Allusion to Eliot's "I have heard the mermaids singing, each to each."

Sonnet 129: This sonnet is Shakespeare's great masterpiece in his collection of sonnets. My silence here is a bow in the presence of Shakespeare's greatness.

Sonnet 130: Experimental. Book metaphor.

Sonnet 131: A sonnet to a Dark Lady.

Sonnet 132: A sonnet for empowerment...also to a Dark Lady.

Sonnet 133: A meditation on our species.

Sonnet 134: On death, identity, and possession.

Sonnet 135: The rare English verb "Jole" is a variation on the verb "Jowl," meaning *to hit* or *to throw.* Cf. *Hamlet*: "That skull had a tongue in it and could sing once. How the knave *jowls* it to the ground, as if 'twere Cain's jawbone, that did the first murder."

Sonnet 136: Another experiment in constrained poetry. This sonnet is built only out of the letters of my name. The last phrase, "jaded devil of lore," is a direct anagram of my name.

Sonnet 137: A meditation on the origin of our sexual tastes.

Sonnet 138: A reflection and elaboration on the Narcissus myth, in which society becomes the narcissistic pool. Contains an allusion to Heidegger's remark, "Language is the house of Being," as well as a reference to Marx's "false consciousness," here couched in the context of relational economies.

Sonnet 139: A breakup sonnet?

Sonnet 140: Tupac was a rap music artist in the late 20th century. "Dasein" is German for "Being," (cf. Heidegger). "Sappho" was an ancient Greek poetess.

Sonnet 141: Ode to Deleuze and Guattari. The playful verb "perlocute" resonates with J. L. Austin's famous triad of locution / illocution / perlocution in his *How to Do Things with Words*. The perlocutionary effects of an utterance reflect intentional audience uptake. Otherwise, the reflection on constraints in this sonnet hints at the question of meaning in constrained poetry.

Sonnet 142: "Psychophant" is a neologism combining "psyche" (Gr., "mind") and "sycophant." A sonnet to a Dark Lady.

Sonnet 143: Birth as a metaphor for pain in love.

Sonnet 144: Evolutionary reflection on fear, survival, solidarity, and success.

Sonnet 145: Some mappings for body parts, human powers, and deities. How much of our thought-structure is metaphorical?

Sonnet 146: Remember the Titans.

Sonnet 147: A sonnet lamenting the absence of a lover.

Sonnet 148: The "panopticon" was an architectural design for a prison created by noted utilitarian philosopher Jeremy Bentham. It was popularized in Foucault's works. The ancient Greek means "all-seen," and the idea was to place a central guard-tower such that prisoners, if not constantly being watched, would develop a consciousness that at any time they were *potentially* being watched. Here the panopticon is plural (*eyes, ghosts, shoulds*). As such, the moral (or "should") function symbolized here only superficially resembles the Super-Ego of psychoanalysis. While potentially condensable to a single figure like a father or a phallic tower, each individual's collection of felt imperatives is practically diffuse in origin and operation, and more resembles Nietzsche's dragon with a thousand scales (or, more abstractly, Foucault's site for the interplay of myriads of forces). As in the Stanford Prison Experiment, the forces involved are not only psychological but also social and physical.

Sonnet 149: We're animals and the world is bloody. An evolutionary spin on what William James calls "tough-minded" versus "tender-minded."

Sonnet 150: "Corps d'esprit" reverses the usual French "Esprit de corps" ("spirit of the body"), so meaning "body of the spirit." The Latin, "homo mensura deae homini" is equally a reversal, and means "man is the measure of the goddesses of man."

Sonnet 151: A look at conscience as a purely social phenomenon.

Sonnet 152: Another Mars/Venus sonnet, echoing sonnets 35-36. "Idiolatry" is a neologism derived from the Greek, meaning "the worship of the self."

Sonnet 153: As Shakespeare's final pairing of sonnets invoke the mythological figure of Cupid, so the tale of Cupid and Psyche inspires my final pair. "Psyche" is Greek for "Mind." The relation between love and mind is a timeless theme (cf. my poem, *inside cupid's psyche*, publication forthcoming).

Sonnet 154: Experimental. I've added a letter to each line to eventually arrive at the first line of the first sonnet of Shakespeare's. "Dasein" is German for "Being." "Terrae," Latin for "lands." "Dies irae," Latin for "day of wrath." "Fantasie," German for fantasy. "Différance," French (via Derrida) for "difference" and "deferment." "Esse" is Latin for "Being.

index of first lines

Sonnet	Author	First Line
16	WS	But wherefore do not you a mightier way
21	JD	Call me Nature's copyist. All I do
29	JD	Can any man cross Jahweh's changeless will?
47	JD	can we philosophize? i love you. i
101	JD	can words describe the color of your soul?
149	WS	Canst thou, O cruel! say I love thee not,
19	JD	clear-flowing time, turn gem to dust and back;
99	JD	"colorless green ideas sleep furiously!"
107	JD	cold white envelops lines of stony black.
9	JD	Come dance with me, spider! Why do you cow-
151	JD	Conscience is born of love, where love is free—
89	JD	consolidate your insecurities.
153	WS	Cupid laid by his brand, and fell asleep:
55	JD	*...dark oneiric anamnesis calls...*
109	JD	darkness oozes all about, around, be-
11	JD	Days dawn on all, and sweet rains fall unbi-
18	JD	Death thou art untrimmed, and owest all to
137	JD	desire's irony is that it hides
19	WS	Devouring Time, blunt thou the lion's paws,
132	JD	disperse the fogs of unreality,
72	JD	dreams number us like pi. runes shift. nights rewind
150	JD	each species has its featured deities—
90	JD	*eli, eli, lama sabachthani?*
87	WS	Farewell! thou art too dear for my possessing,
78	JD	fixation is the problem—need & greed—
10	JD	For Shame! Not Anger, Guilt or Pride, nor sad
10	WS	For shame! deny that thou bear'st love to any,
1	WS	FROM fairest creatures we desire increase,
98	WS	From you have I been absent in the spring,
33	WS	Full many a glorious morning have I seen
85	JD	god, love, & money are the masks we wear—
121	JD	have i just sinned? have i been indiscreet?
145	JD	...Head, Heart and Gut are passing *wine,*
28	WS	How can I then return in happy plight,
38	WS	How can my Muse want subject to invent,
48	WS	How careful was I, when I took my way,
67	JD	how do we humans treat the earth?
50	WS	How heavy do I journey on the way,
97	WS	How like a winter hath my absence been
128	WS	How oft, when thou, my music, music play'st,

Sonnet	Author	First Line
95	WS	How sweet and lovely dost thou make the shame
50	JD	I bear your fears, your tears, your late *adieu*;
97	JD	i chase my single arc from dark to dark
82	WS	I grant thou wert not married to my Muse
152	JD	I guess this is goodbye, my goddess-girl.
119	JD	i love myself—i love this store of days
105	JD	I love you, neighbor, like I love myself.
120	JD	i made myself a promise to be true.
43	JD	i met your eyes, i thought, i met your mind:
83	WS	I never saw that you did painting need
143	JD	i scream my way into maturity—
56	JD	i soared. eye-sored, i (sword, ice or dice), sort
115	JD	i took the crown from the tyrant's head. i spread—
140	JD	i walk among symbols & figures & signs.
138	JD	i will not thank you for your flattery,
153	JD	I, Cupid, pricked myself with my own brand,
154	JD	i,
17	JD	i'm sure
37	JD	*...ideas are whores, but wisdom is a maid...*
136	JD	if ever i loved, i loved life. if ev-
133	JD	if everyone remembered everything,
111	JD	if i could pluck the stars from out your eyes,
124	WS	If my dear love were but the child of state,
59	JD	if nothing's new beneath this burning star,
44	WS	If the dull substance of my flesh were thought,
59	WS	If there be nothing new, but that which is
32	WS	If thou survive my well-contented day,
136	WS	If thy soul cheque thee that I come so near,
141	WS	In faith, I do not love thee with mine eyes,
152	WS	In loving thee thou know'st I am forsworn,
127	WS	In the old age black was not counted fair,
38	JD	in you i find my union with all things.
9	WS	Is it for fear to wet a widow's eye
61	WS	Is it thy will thy image should keep open
25	JD	LET KINGS & SOLDIERS PEN THEIR HISTORIES
36	WS	Let me confess that we two must be twain,
116	WS	Let me not to the marriage of true minds
105	WS	Let not my love be call'd idolatry,
25	WS	Let those who are in favour with their stars
71	JD	let us go then, You and I, and add an-

Sonnet	Author	First Line
60	WS	Like as the waves make towards the pebbled shore,
118	WS	Like as, to make our appetites more keen,
143	WS	Lo! as a careful housewife runs to catch
7	WS	Lo! in the orient when the gracious light
3	JD	Look in this pool—within the face you're viewing
3	WS	Look in thy glass, and tell the face thou viewest
7	JD	Look to the Orient where soft-red dawns
26	WS	Lord of my love, to whom in vassalage
142	WS	Love is my sin and thy dear virtue hate,
151	WS	Love is too young to know what conscience is;
46	WS	Mine eye and heart are at a mortal war
24	WS	Mine eye hath play'd the painter and hath stell'd
8	WS	Music to hear, why hear'st thou music sadly?
8	JD	Music? My bow has hovered o'er your strings,
106	JD	my beauty lives. why do you then lament
84	JD	my fashion-forward style of unity is mine alone—
22	WS	My glass shall not persuade me I am old,
20	JD	my jungle jury echoes, "onan...o...."
83	JD	my letters are but pointless blots & marks,
147	WS	My love is as a fever, longing still
102	WS	My love is strengthen'd, though more weak in seeming;
130	WS	My mistress' eyes are nothing like the sun;
32	JD	my not-ness: monotonous unravelling
134	JD	my time on earth has flown invisible
85	WS	My tongue-tied Muse in manners holds her still,
110	JD	my wisdom's come from doing foolish things—
125	JD	new tasks confront my existential stores,
14	JD	night-swimming sky-vault summer pangs past
79	JD	no cup is large enough to hold the sea,
71	WS	No longer mourn for me when I am dead
35	WS	No more be grieved at that which thou hast done:
123	WS	No, Time, thou shalt not boast that I do change:
14	WS	Not from the stars do I my judgment pluck;
55	WS	Not marble, nor the gilded monuments
107	WS	Not mine own fears, nor the prophetic soul
26	JD	*o domina, dicte et facam quod*
81	JD	O Ilium, shake spirits from the graves
148	WS	O me, what eyes hath Love put in my head,
126	WS	O thou, my lovely boy, who in thy power
101	WS	O truant Muse, what shall be thy amends

Sonnet	Author	First Line
139	WS	O, call not me to justify the wrong
111	WS	O, for my sake do you with Fortune chide,
150	WS	O, from what power hast thou this powerful might
80	WS	O, how I faint when I of you do write,
54	WS	O, how much more doth beauty beauteous seem
39	WS	O, how thy worth with manners may I sing,
72	WS	O, lest the world should task you to recite
109	WS	O, never say that I was false of heart,
13	WS	O, that you were yourself! but, love, you are
82	JD	once coined, a word or metaphor or phrase
48	JD	...or so they say. but our love knows better.
81	WS	Or I shall live your epitaph to make,
114	WS	Or whether doth my mind, being crown'd with you,
116	JD	our bodies find new kinds of intercourse.
87	JD	our cultural unconscious dreams of wealth:
144	JD	our fears are best addressed as embryos—
51	JD	our truth lies here & there & everywhere:
69	JD	our words commune and, in their surplus, feed
146	WS	Poor soul, the centre of my sinful earth,
36	JD	queen takes king...mate...girl meets boy: his turns hers. womb
53	JD	*quid tua substantia, fabrica?*
54	JD	rose-boughs mature anew sweet, dubious dreams.
89	WS	Say that thou didst forsake me for some fault,
62	JD	self-ish in every body i've become
139	JD	separate and equal, let us live our lives,
18	WS	Shall I compare thee to a summer's day?
91	JD	she drinks her wine. he drinks his gatorade.
127	JD	should I compare you to a summer day?
62	WS	Sin of self-love possesseth all mine eye
65	JD	since "stabbed," or "hanged," or "drowned," or "overdosed"
65	WS	Since brass, nor stone, nor earth, nor boundless sea,
113	WS	Since I left you, mine eye is in my mind;
88	JD	since they won't let me live here anymore,
52	WS	So am I as the rich, whose blessed key
75	WS	So are you to my thoughts as food to life,
21	WS	So is it not with me as with that Muse
117	JD	so kick my ass and take my name. okay.
78	WS	So oft have I invoked thee for my Muse
93	WS	So shall I live, supposing thou art true,
134	WS	So, now I have confess'd that he is thine,

Sonnet	Author	First Line
91	WS	Some glory in their birth, some in their skill,
96	WS	Some say thy fault is youth, some wantonness;
35	JD	still a moment for your stillborn deeds, for
24	JD	still life fruit evil good of knowing you.
33	JD	Sunday: hail christ or helios: which dawn?
56	WS	Sweet love, renew thy force; be it not said
121	WS	'Tis better to be vile than vile esteem'd,
40	WS	Take all my loves, my love, yea, take them all;
57	JD	take me, your own love slave. have me. *also,*
58	WS	That god forbid that made me first your slave,
70	WS	That thou art blamed shall not be thy defect,
42	WS	That thou hast her, it is not all my grief,
73	WS	That time of year thou mayst in me behold
120	WS	That you were once unkind befriends me now,
95	JD	the "lie" that hides my muscles is my skin.
64	JD	The ancient slab is loosened from the wall;
86	JD	The center of your soul is my abode.
130	JD	the cover always permeates the page,
60	JD	the deep blue groundswells heave & sigh. oceans
13	JD	the earth and all generations are your
129	WS	The expense of spirit in a waste of shame
99	WS	The forward violet thus did I chide:
73	JD	The Grim Surveyor lays on me his line,
154	WS	The little Love-god lying once asleep
77	JD	the mirror is the place you find your way,
63	JD	the *now* of how i feel does not depend
45	WS	The other two, slight air and purging fire,
100	JD	the tentacles of will entangle us:
2	JD	The tessellated snowflake lands its slender
128	JD	the words you use show where you're coming from.
74	JD	the world is forced to whisper when it snows.
90	WS	Then hate me when thou wilt; if ever, now;
6	WS	Then let not winter's ragged hand deface
92	JD	these bursts of passion steal my "self" away.
76	JD	these duodactylic & risible lines
142	JD	they say you never get a second chance
112	JD	they stamped my forehead with the mark of cain
94	WS	They that have power to hurt and will do none,
132	WS	Thine eyes I love, and they, as pitying me,
28	JD	this web of nerves is our intelligence—

Sonnet	Author	First Line
5	WS	Those hours, that with gentle work did frame
115	WS	Those lines that I before have writ do lie,
145	WS	Those lips that Love's own hand did make
69	WS	Those parts of thee that the world's eye doth view
41	WS	Those petty wrongs that liberty commits,
131	WS	Thou art as tyrannous, so as thou art,
137	WS	Thou blind fool, Love, what dost thou to mine eyes,
135	JD	Though I beseech, you'll have your morning "Jole."
51	WS	Thus can my love excuse the slow offence
68	WS	Thus is his cheek the map of days outworn,
31	WS	Thy bosom is endeared with all hearts,
122	WS	Thy gift, thy tables, are within my brain
77	WS	Thy glass will show thee how thy beauties wear,
5	JD	'Tick...tick...drip...drip...' sings your spring of beauty—
113	JD	till i met you, my "i" was in my "mine."
123	JD	time's sickle pops off fickle fatherhoods,
66	WS	Tired with all these, for restful death I cry,
6	JD	To catch this catalyst? It's harder than
148	JD	to go where there is wisdom on the wind,
104	WS	To me, fair friend, you never can be old,
96	JD	translation is a land where much gets lost.
66	JD	trapped in this web of names, for choice i yearn,
45	JD	truth and water, too, grip her sighing life. I
34	JD	Twelve tribes, apostles, months, chromatic tones:
144	WS	Two loves I have of comfort and despair,
44	JD	two witnesses—the spirit and the blood—
4	WS	Unthrifty loveliness, why dost thou spend
86	WS	Was it the proud full sail of his great verse,
68	JD	we wear our wigs and usually forget
22	JD	We've grown so close in love that I don't know
27	WS	Weary with toil, I haste me to my bed,
125	WS	Were 't aught to me I bore the canopy,
53	WS	What is your substance, whereof are you made,
119	WS	What potions have I drunk of Siren tears,
58	JD	whatever victimizing super-ego
108	WS	What's in the brain that ink may character
108	JD	when "pro," i'm -scribed by all my -creations.
61	JD	when drowsy thoughts like dew condense on you
2	WS	When forty winters shall beseige thy brow,
15	WS	When I consider every thing that grows

Sonnet	Author	First Line
12	WS	When I do count the clock that tells the time,
64	WS	When I have seen by Time's fell hand defaced
106	WS	When in the chronicle of wasted time
43	WS	When most I wink, then do mine eyes best see,
138	WS	When my love swears that she is made of truth
15	JD	when photosynthesizing next to you
30	JD	when some wet lore-drop surfaces to thought,
88	WS	When thou shalt be disposed to set me light,
30	WS	When to the sessions of sweet silent thought
12	JD	when worlds tick to my java-eddy spoons
131	JD	when you have called on all your other gods
114	JD	when you're some random bits of stimuli,
29	WS	When, in disgrace with fortune and men's eyes,
39	JD	when, love, we make these vows, what do we mean:
100	WS	Where art thou, Muse, that thou forget'st so long
79	WS	Whilst I alone did call upon thy aid,
84	WS	Who is it that says most? which can say more
102	JD	who is this author-ideality
17	WS	Who will believe my verse in time to come,
135	WS	Whoever hath her wish, thou hast thy 'Will,'
34	WS	Why didst thou promise such a beauteous day,
76	WS	Why is my verse so barren of new pride,
94	JD	with power comes responsibility.
27	JD	working the soil as dawn's red lord ascends,
70	JD	you don't want fame or a great name, do you?
98	JD	you fuck me. we don't make love anymore.
42	JD	you thaw to me, like a first frost on ripe
147	JD	your absence is my fever: steely sky,
118	JD	your life-events flow into you like drugs.
112	WS	Your love and pity doth the impression fill
75	JD	your love is my identity's undoing,
122	JD	your mind, o humankind, does not compute.
1	JD	Your trembling petals when bedecked with dews,
41	JD	your virtue's vicious circle orbits me.
31	JD	you're ore. gold. you were here before *homo*
103	JD	you've heard, "in the beginning was the Word."
129	JD